ASIA BOND MONITOR
JUNE 2024

Contents

Emerging East Asian Local Currency Bond Markets: A Regional Update

Emerging East Asian Local Currency Bond Markets: A Regional Update

Executive Summary

Recent Developments in Financial Conditions in Emerging East Asia

Between 1 March and 31 May, financial conditions weakened in emerging East Asia on a delay in the expected rate cut by the United States (US) Federal Reserve.[1] A slower-than-expected disinflation path supported the likelihood of higher-for-longer interest rates and pushed up short-term and long-term bond yields in both advanced economies and regional markets. This led to bond outflows from regional markets amounting to USD20 billion in March–April.

The delay in the Federal Reserve's expected rate cut and hawkish tones from its officials contributed to weakening financial conditions in regional markets during the review period. Regional currencies depreciated by 1.8% (simple average) and 1.1% (gross-domestic-product-weighted) against the US dollar. Credit default swap spreads widened in five out of seven markets in which data are available. While most regional equity markets recorded gains during the review period on domestic factors, Association of Southeast Asian Nations (ASEAN) equity markets witnessed USD4.7 billion outflows.

With lingering uncertainty over the path of disinflation, risks to regional financial conditions are tilted to the downside. Uncertainties regarding US monetary policy could support a strong US dollar, leading to additional outflows from emerging East Asia and currency weakness. Regional domestic monetary authorities may face pressure to hold interest rates higher for a longer period to safeguard their respective currencies. Heightened geopolitical risks, trade tensions, and adverse weather events could further add inflationary pressure via rising freight costs, supply chain disruptions, and higher food prices.

Recent Developments in Local Currency Bond Markets in Emerging East Asia

Emerging East Asia's local currency (LCY) bond market expanded 1.4% quarter-on-quarter (q-o-q) to reach a size of USD24.7 trillion at the end of the first quarter (Q1) of 2024. The region's bond market expansion slowed slightly in Q1 2024 compared to growth of 1.8% q-o-q in the previous quarter. The slower expansion was largely due to deep contractions in government bond issuance in the People's Republic of China (PRC) and Hong Kong, China, which outpaced increased issuance in other emerging East Asian markets. Meanwhile, regional corporate bonds outstanding edged up 1.2% q-o-q in Q1 2024, supported by robust corporate issuance in the PRC and Hong Kong, China that followed the PRC's introduction of easing measures to boost the domestic economy. Outstanding LCY bonds among members of the ASEAN totaled USD2.2 trillion at the end of March, accounting for 8.9% of the emerging East Asian total.

LCY bond issuance in emerging East Asia totaled USD2.2 trillion in Q1 2024, declining 9.0% q-o-q as issuance fell for both government and corporate bonds. Government bond issuance fell 18.1% q-o-q to USD853.8 billion, driven by a contraction in issuance in the PRC from a high base in the previous quarter when the government frontloaded part of its 2024 borrowing quota to boost economic growth. Regional LCY corporate bond issuance contracted 1.9% q-o-q to USD822.1 billion as high interest rates suppressed borrowing in most regional markets. ASEAN markets' LCY bond issuance amounted to USD538.6 billion in Q1 2024, comprising 24.2% of the regional issuance total.

---

[1] Emerging East Asia is defined to include member states of the Association of Southeast Asian Nations (ASEAN) plus the People's Republic of China; Hong Kong, China; and the Republic of Korea.

Treasury bonds outstanding and issuances in emerging East Asia remained concentrated in medium- to long-term maturities. By the end of Q1 2024, the size-weighted average tenor of outstanding Treasury bonds was 8.2 years, while that for Treasury bond issuance during the quarter was 7.7 years. Over half (52.6%) of outstanding Treasury bonds at the end of March had maturities longer than 5 years; the corresponding share for Treasury bond issuance during the quarter was 54.7%.

Emerging East Asian LCY Treasury bonds remained largely held by passive investor groups such as banks and insurance and pension funds. At the end of March, banks held the largest average share of LCY Treasury bonds across all regional markets (36.6%), followed by insurance and pension funds (28.9%). Meanwhile, Treasury bond markets in Indonesia and the Republic of Korea had the most diversified investor profiles in emerging East Asia.

Recent Developments in ASEAN+3 Sustainable Bond Markets

The ASEAN+3 sustainable bond market expanded 21.4% on an annual basis to reach a size of USD805.9 billion at the end of March.[2] Year-on-year growth in the ASEAN+3 sustainable bond market exceeded growth in both the European Union 20 (EU-20) (20.4%) and the overall global market (17.7%). ASEAN+3 continued to account for the world's second-largest regional sustainable bond market at the end of Q1 2024 with a global share of 18.9%, trailing only the EU-20's 37.6%. Despite the expansion, sustainable bonds outstanding comprised only 2.1% of ASEAN+3's total bond market at the end of March, lagging the EU-20's corresponding share of 7.3%.

Sustainable bond issuance in ASEAN+3 contracted 13.3% q-o-q to USD49.7 billion in Q1 2024 on expectations of higher-for-longer interest rates in the US and throughout the region. LCY-denominated bonds accounted for 79.3% of the quarterly issuance total, which was less than the LCY-denominated share of 96.4% for general bond market issuance. Short-term financing (maturities of 5 years or less) accounted for 77.4% of ASEAN+3 sustainable bond issuance in Q1 2024, while the size-weighted average tenor of total quarterly issuance was 5.0 years in ASEAN+3, compared with 9.7 years in the EU-20.

---

[2] ASEAN+3 is defined to include member states of the Association of Southeast Asian Nations (ASEAN) plus the People's Republic of China; Hong Kong, China; Japan; and the Republic of Korea.

Developments in Regional Financial Conditions

Financial conditions in emerging East Asia slightly weakened from 1 March to 31 May on a delay in the expected rate cut in the United States (US).[1] The widely expected US rate cut in June was delayed due to a slower-than-expected disinflation path and related uncertainty. Higher-for-longer interest rates in the US pushed up bond yields in both advanced economies and emerging East Asia, and contributed to a strengthening US dollar and widening risk premiums in most regional markets during the review period. Association of Southeast Asian Nations (ASEAN) markets recorded bond and equity portfolio outflows during the review period. Risks to regional financial conditions remain tilted to the downside, as lingering geopolitical risks and weather-related shocks add uncertainty to the future inflation path and monetary policy adjustments.

Local currency (LCY) sovereign bond yields rose for both 2-year and 10-year tenors in major advanced economies from 1 March to 31 May, largely driven by persistent inflation and expectations of higher-for-longer interest rates (**Table A**). The timing of policy rate cuts in the US remains uncertain due to sticky inflation that lingers above the 2% target. In the euro area, the central bank proceeded with a widely expected rate cut in June; however, uncertainty persists with regard to future monetary policy direction after that. In the case of Japan, the rise in yields was driven by the Bank of Japan's (BOJ) tightening monetary stance as it ended its quantitative and qualitative easing program in March (with a prospect for further tightening).

During the review period, 2-year and 10-year government bond yields in the US rose on uncertainty in the timing and magnitude of expected rate cuts. The slow decline in inflation and ongoing geopolitical tensions generated uncertainty about the path of inflation. During the review period, the Federal Reserve turned hawkish about possible interest rate cuts. At its 19–20 March Federal Open Market Committee (FOMC) meeting, the

Table A: Changes in Financial Conditions in Major Advanced Economies and Select Emerging East Asian Markets from 1 March to 31 May 2024

	2-Year Government Bond Yield (bps)	10-Year Government Bond Yield (bps)	5-Year Credit Default Swap Spread (bps)	Equity Index (%)	FX Rate (%)
Major Advanced Economies					
Germany	21	25	–	1.8	0.1
Japan	22	35	1	1.7	(4.6)
United States	34	32	–	2.7	–
Select Emerging East Asian Markets					
People's Republic of China	(28)	(6)	(2)	2.0	(0.6)
Hong Kong, China	19	3	–	9.0	0.1
Indonesia	44	28	3	(4.7)	(3.4)
Republic of Korea	(0.2)	10	3	(0.2)	(3.9)
Malaysia	9	4	8	3.8	0.8
Philippines	19	51	6	(7.0)	(4.3)
Singapore	15	25	–	6.4	(0.5)
Thailand	25	25	1	(1.6)	(2.3)
Viet Nam	64	52	(10)	0.3	(3.2)

( ) = negative, – = not available, bps = basis points, FX = foreign exchange.
Note: FX rates are presented against the United States dollar. A positive (negative) value for the FX rate indicates the appreciation (depreciation) of the local currency against the United States dollar.
Source: *AsianBondsOnline* calculations based on Bloomberg LP data.

[1] Emerging East Asia is defined to include member states of the Association of Southeast Asian Nations (ASEAN) plus the People's Republic of China; Hong Kong, China; and the Republic of Korea.

Federal Reserve held steady the federal funds target rate range at 5.25%–5.50% and announced it still expected three rate cuts in 2024. This supported expectations that the Federal Reserve would make its first rate cut in June, with the CME FedWatch Tool's probability of a June rate cut increasing from 50.8% on 18 March to 67.4% on 20 March. However, the March FOMC meeting minutes, released on 10 April, noted uncertainty over the persistence of high inflation, as data releases did not support the view that inflation was heading sustainably toward its goal. Federal Reserve officials further bolstered their hawkish tone in subsequent pronouncements, reinforcing expectations that the Federal Reserve did not expect to reduce its policy rate until it had greater confidence that inflation was moving toward the 2% target.[2] During the 30 April–1 May FOMC meeting, Chairman Jerome Powell ruled out the possibility of a rate hike at the June FOMC meeting, noting that inflation had not progressed toward its goal. Moreover, on 11 May, Federal Reserve Governor Michelle Bowman said that she saw no reason for the Federal Reserve to cut rates in 2024. As a result, the likelihood of the first rate cut in June, as indicated by the CME FedWatch Tool, plunged from 67.4% on 20 March to 9.3% on 1 May and further to 4.4% on 31 May (**Figure A**). During its 11–12 June

Figure A: Probability of the First 25 Basis Points Rate Cut at the June, September, or November 2024 Federal Open Market Committee Meeting

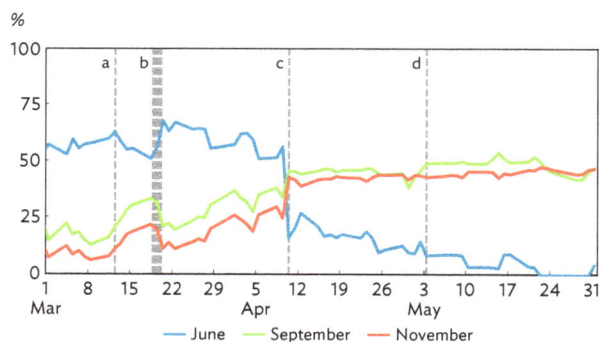

FOMC = Federal Open Market Committee.
Note: Data are as of 31 May 2024.
a Release of higher-than-expected February consumer price inflation.
b March FOMC meeting with the Federal Reserve dotplot indicating three rate cuts still likely in 2024.
c Release of March FOMC minutes with participants indicating the need for greater confidence to bring inflation toward its 2% goal.
d Release of April nonfarm payroll employment, which fell sharply from March level.
Source: CME FedWatch Tool.

FOMC meeting, the Federal Reserve left the policy rate unchanged, as widely expected, and revised the federal funds target rate forecast from three cuts each in 2024, 2025, and 2026 to one cut in 2024 and four cuts each in 2025 and 2026. On 31 May, the market was pricing in the probability of the Federal Reserve's first rate cut of 25 basis points (bps) occurring in September at 47.0%, up from 14.9% on 1 March, and occurring in November at 46.6%, up from 7.3% on 1 March (Figure A).

A sound economic performance and slow progress toward the Federal Reserve's 2% inflation target in the US supported the delay in rate cuts. Consumer price inflation continued to tick downward, coming in at 3.3% year-on-year (y-o-y) in May versus 3.4% y-o-y in April and 3.5% y-o-y in March. Core inflation, which excludes volatile items such as food and energy, also trended down to 3.4% y-o-y in May from 3.6% y-o-y in April and 3.8% y-o-y in March. However, disinflation progress has been slow amid pending upside risks from geopolitical tensions and adverse weather conditions. The Federal Reserve raised its 2024 and 2025 Personal Consumption Expenditures inflation forecasts in June to 2.6% and 2.3%, respectively, from 2.4% and 2.2% in March. While disinflation progress has been slow, the US economy remains sound. Although annualized gross domestic product (GDP) growth slowed to 1.3% in the first quarter (Q1) of 2024 from 3.4% in the previous quarter, in March the Federal Reserve upgraded its GDP projections for 2024 and 2025 to 2.1% and 2.0%, respectively, from projections of 1.4% and 1.8% made in December. US GDP forecasts were left unchanged at the June FOMC meeting. Meanwhile, the unemployment rate remained low at 3.9% in April and 4.0% in May. On 7 June, the release of nonfarm payroll data showed additions had improved to 272,000 in May from 165,000 in April. The combination of a strong labor market and slow progress in steering inflation toward a sustainable level led the Federal Reserve to extend its hawkish stance.

Government bond yields rose in the euro area during the review period, reflecting uncertainty about the European Central Bank's (ECB) monetary policy path following its rate cut in June. The ECB kept its key interest rates unchanged at its 10–11 April meeting, with the minutes indicating that a rate cut at its June meeting was likely if growth and inflation developments

---

[2] These include talks in April made by Federal Reserve Governor Michelle Bowman, Federal Reserve Bank of Dallas President Lorie Logan, and Federal Reserve Bank of Kansas City President Jeff Schmid.

were in line with ECB projections and inflation "was converging to target in a sustained manner." On 14 May, Dutch central bank Governor Klaas Knot stated that it would be appropriate to remove some monetary restrictions if growth and policy developments remained on track. On 15 May, Bank of France Governor Francois Villeroy de Galhau said that the initial rate cut would likely take place in June. On 21 May, ECB President Christine Lagarde noted that if incoming data confirm the ECB's view that the 2% inflation target is within reach, then it is highly likely that the ECB would cut rates in June.

The ECB, as widely expected, reduced by 25 bps its key policy rates in its 6 June meeting but noted the magnitude and timing of subsequent rate cuts remain uncertain amid upside risks to the inflation outlook. Such risks include uncertainty in food prices due to extreme weather events and uncertainty in oil prices due to wider conflict in the Middle East. Annual inflation in the euro area trended down to 2.4% in March and April from 2.6% in February and 2.8% in January. The ECB's revised projection for 2024 indicated that inflation is stickier than previously expected, with 2024 inflation projected at 2.5% in June compared with a 2.3% projection in March. The corresponding inflation forecast for 2025 was also raised to 2.2% from 2.0%. The European Commission's inflation forecasts for the euro area were also revised down to 2.5% and 2.1% for 2024 and 2025, respectively, from 2.7% and 2.2%. Meanwhile, the economic outlook remains robust. GDP growth rose to 0.4% y-o-y in Q1 2024 from 0.2% y-o-y in the previous quarter. In June, the ECB upgraded its 2024 GDP growth forecast to 0.9% from 0.6% in March, largely due to robust wage growth driving household spending. May inflation rose slightly to 2.6% y-o-y, confirming uncertainty over the future monetary policy path.

During the review period, Japan's bond yields rose on the BOJ normalizing its monetary policy. Japan's inflation remains above the BOJ's 2% target, with consumer price inflation trending down from 2.8% y-o-y in February to 2.7% y-o-y in March and 2.5% y-o-y in April. In its April meeting, the BOJ adjusted upward its 2024 and 2025 inflation forecasts to 2.8% and 1.9%, respectively, from January forecasts of 2.4% and 1.8%. At its 18–19 March meeting, the BOJ ended its quantitative and qualitative monetary easing by ceasing yield curve control, the negative interest rate, and the asset purchase program of exchange-traded funds and real estate investment trusts. The central bank announced the shift to using the short-term interest rate (uncollateralized overnight

range) as its primary monetary policy tool and decided to increase the range of the uncollateralized overnight call rate to 0.0%–0.1% from a range of –0.1% to 0.0%. The BOJ will gradually reduce and eventually end its purchase of commercial paper and corporate bonds in about a year. In its announcement of the change in its monetary policy framework, the BOJ stated that its large-scale monetary easing program had fulfilled its purpose, judging that the previous inflation target of 2.0% could now be achieved in a stable and sustainable manner.

The BOJ also signaled the possibility of further tightening. On 8 May, BOJ Governor Kazuo Ueda said that it would be appropriate to reduce the Japanese Government Bond purchasing plan as the BOJ normalizes its monetary policy. In the Summary of Opinions at the Monetary Policy Meeting released on 9 May, the BOJ stated that the degree of monetary policy accommodation will be adjusted once "the outlook for economic activity and prices will be realized and underlying inflation will increase." Per the BOJ statement, if the current forecasts are achieved, the expected BOJ policy rate will be higher than what the market is currently pricing in. Further, at its 13-14 June monetary policy meeting, the BOJ left unchanged its policy rate but announced that it would begin to reduce Japanese Government Bond purchases, subject to a finalized plan to be released at its July monetary policy meeting.

LCY government bond yields in emerging East Asia rose for 2-year and 10-year tenors across the region, largely on persistent domestic inflation in a few regional markets in recent months and rising yields in advanced markets. The persistent inflation was related to weather disturbances and geopolitical tensions that added pressure to commodity and food prices (**Figure B**). Persistent inflation coupled with the Federal Reserve's delay in cutting rates to support expectations of possible higher-for-longer interest rates in regional markets (**Table B**). In April, Bank Indonesia raised its policy rate by 25 bps to 6.25% to safeguard its currency. Meanwhile, other regional central banks signaled delays in possible rate cuts. Bank of Korea Governor Rhee Chang-yong noted that, while there were expectations for interest rate cuts in the second half of the year, uncertainty over their timing had risen. The Bank of Thailand maintained the policy rate on 10 April at 2.50% despite the government's pressure for a rate cut, noting that inflation would gradually move toward the target range by the end of 2024. In March and April, regional bond markets witnessed net portfolio

Figure B: Inflation in Major Advanced Economies and Select Emerging East Asian Markets

%, y-o-y

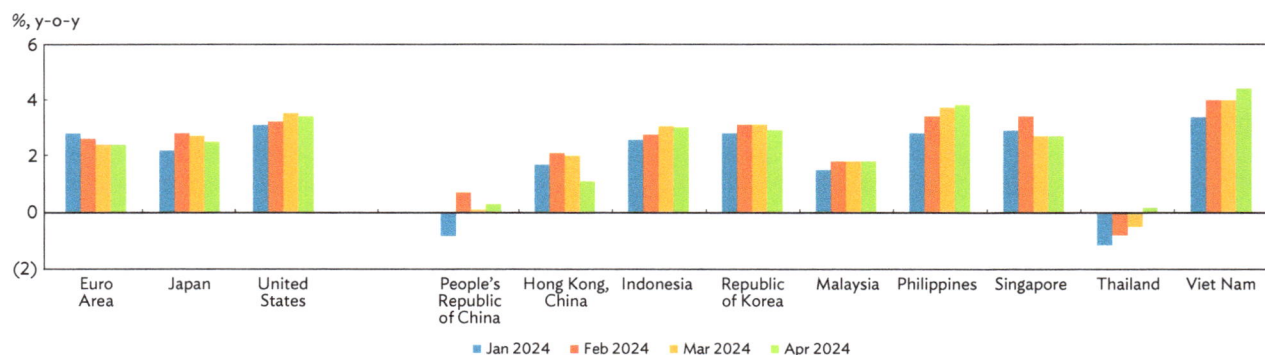

y-o-y = year-on-year.
Sources: Various local sources.

Table B: Changes in Monetary Stances in Major Advanced Economies and Select Emerging East Asian Markets

Economy	Policy Rate 1-May-2023 (%)	Rate Change (%)													Policy Rate 31-May-2024 (%)	Change in Policy Rates (basis points)
		May- 2023	Jun- 2023	Jul- 2023	Aug- 2023	Sep- 2023	Oct- 2023	Nov- 2023	Dec- 2023	Jan- 2024	Feb- 2024	Mar- 2024	Apr- 2024	May- 2024		
Euro Area	3.00	↑0.25	↑0.25		↑0.25	↑0.25									4.00	↑ 100
Japan	(0.10)											↑0.20			0.10	↑ 20
United Kingdom	4.25	↑0.25	↑0.50		↑0.25										5.25	↑ 100
United States	5.00	↑0.25		↑0.25											5.50	↑ 50
People's Republic of China	2.75		↓0.10		↓0.15										2.50	↓ 25
Indonesia	5.75						↑0.25						↑0.25		6.25	↑ 50
Republic of Korea	3.50														3.50	◆ 0
Malaysia	2.75	↑0.25													3.00	↑ 25
Philippines	6.25						↑0.25								6.50	↑ 25
Singapore	–														–	–
Thailand	1.75	↑0.25			↑0.25	↑0.25									2.50	↑ 75
Viet Nam	5.50	↓0.50	↓0.50												4.50	↓ 100

( ) = negative, ◆ = no change, – = no data.

Notes:
1. Data coverage is from 1 May 2023 to 31 May 2024.
2. For the People's Republic of China, the data used in the chart are for the 1-year medium-term lending facility rate. While the 1-year benchmark lending rate is the official policy rate of the People's Bank of China, market players use the 1-year medium-term lending facility rate as a guide for the bank's monetary policy direction.
3. For Japan and the United States, the upper bound of the policy rate target range is reported on the table.
4. The up (down) arrow for Singapore signifies monetary policy tightening (loosening) by its central bank. The Monetary Authority of Singapore utilizes the Singapore dollar nominal effective exchange rate to guide its monetary policy.

Sources: Various central bank websites.

outflows of USD20.0 billion due to a collective rise in bond yields and subdued risk appetite over expected higher-for-longer interest rates (**Figure C**). One exception to this rising yield trend was the People's Republic of China (PRC), where bond yields fell on low inflation and monetary easing to support economic growth and the property market.

Emerging East Asian currencies weakened against the US dollar during the review period, with the dollar strengthening after the Federal Reserve delayed its expected rate cut. Regional currencies weakened by 1.8% (simple average) and 1.1% (GDP-weighted average) from 1 March to 31 May. The currency deprecations mostly happened in March and April, while some strengthening

Figure C: Foreign Capital Flows in Select Emerging East Asian Local Currency Bond Markets

USD billion

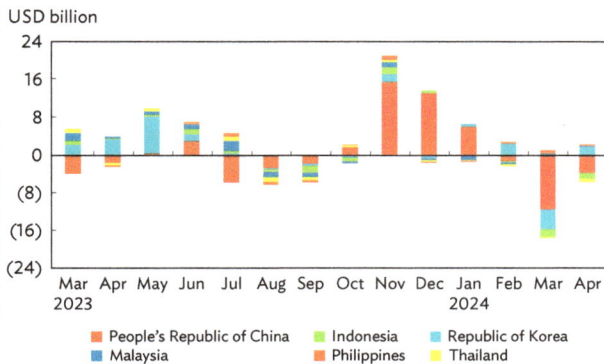

( ) = negative, USD = United States dollar.

Notes:
1. The Republic of Korea and Thailand provided data on bond flows. For the People's Republic of China, Indonesia, Malaysia, and the Philippines, month-on-month changes in foreign holdings of local currency government bonds were used as a proxy for bond flows.
2. Data are as of 30 April 2024.
3. Figures were computed based on 30 April 2024 exchange rates and do not include currency effects.

Sources: People's Republic of China (Bloomberg LP); Indonesia (Directorate General of Budget Financing and Risk Management, Ministry of Finance); Republic of Korea (Financial Supervisory Service); Malaysia (Bank Negara Malaysia); Philippines (Bureau of the Treasury); and Thailand (Thai Bond Market Association).

Figure D: Currency Exchange Rate Movements in Select Emerging East Asian Markets

1 Jan 2024 = 100

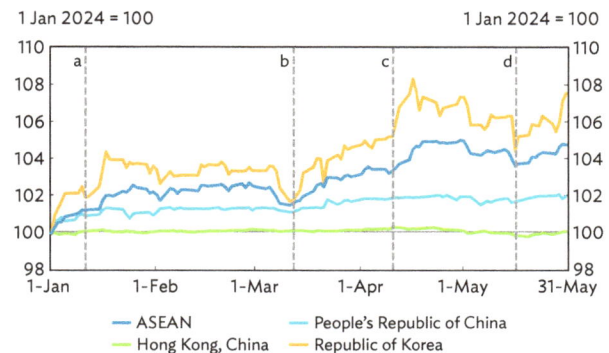

ASEAN = Association of Southeast Asian Nations.

a Federal Reserve Bank of Cleveland President Loretta Mester says March is probably too early for a rate cut.
b February United States consumer price inflation is reported higher than in the previous month.
c Minutes of 19–20 March Federal Open Market Committee meeting released with participants noting inflation remains persistently high.
d Federal Reserve Bank of Minneapolis President Neel Kashkari says rate cuts should be kept on hold.

Notes:
1. ASEAN comprises the markets of Indonesia, Malaysia, the Philippines, Singapore, Thailand, and Viet Nam.
2. Data are as of 31 May 2024.
3. A higher level indicates currency depreciation against the United States dollar.

Source: *AsianBondsOnline* calculations based on Bloomberg LP data.

was observed in early May following the release of easing US April inflation data compared to March, as well as a large drop in nonfarm payroll additions (**Figure D**). This news raised optimism that the Federal Reserve might consider a rate cut within the year.

Similarly, risk premiums, as measured by credit default swap (CDS) spreads, widened in most markets in the region between 1 March and 31 May. The CDS spread increased by a simple average of 1.4 bps, but narrowed 0.9 bps when GDP-weighted, during the review period. Risk premiums widened across most regional markets in March and April following the announced delay in US rate cuts (**Figure E**). However, CDS spreads narrowed in May as expectations of higher-for-longer interest rates in the US were tempered by data for April nonfarm payroll additions and inflation, both of which were down from March levels. Viet Nam witnessed a large reduction in its risk premium as it was kept on the watchlist in March 2024 for a possible upgrade to secondary emerging market classification by FTSE Russell. The next FTSE Russell review will be in September 2024.

Figure E: Changes in Credit Default Swap Spreads in Select Emerging East Asian Markets (senior 5-year)

Basis points

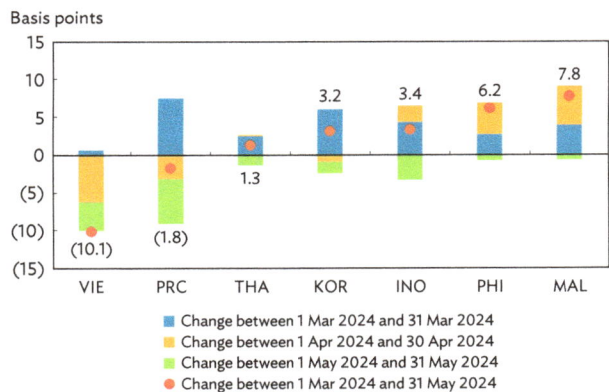

( ) = negative; INO = Indonesia; KOR = Republic of Korea; MAL = Malaysia; PHI = Philippines; PRC = People's Republic of China; THA = Thailand; VIE = Viet Nam.

Note: The numbers above (below) each bar refer to the change in spreads between 1 March 2024 and 31 May 2024.

Source: *AsianBondsOnline* calculations based on Bloomberg LP data.

Figure F: Changes in Equity Indexes in Select Emerging East Asian Markets

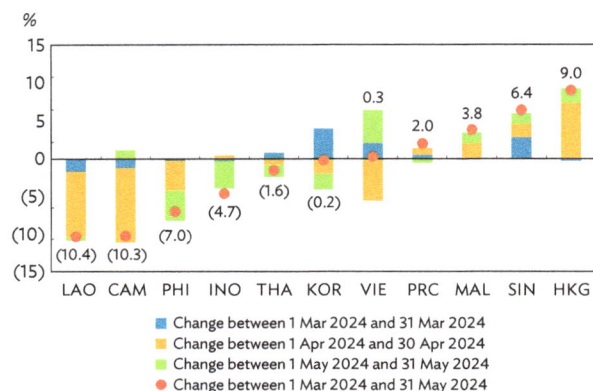

( ) = negative; CAM = Cambodia; HKG = Hong Kong, China; INO = Indonesia; KOR = Republic of Korea; LAO = Lao People's Democratic Republic; MAL = Malaysia; PHI = Philippines; PRC = People's Republic of China; SIN = Singapore; THA = Thailand; VIE = Viet Nam.

Note: The numbers above (below) each bar refer to the change between 1 March 2024 and 31 May 2024.

Source: *AsianBondsOnline* calculations based on Bloomberg LP data.

Figure G: Foreign Capital Flows in Select Emerging East Asian Equity Markets

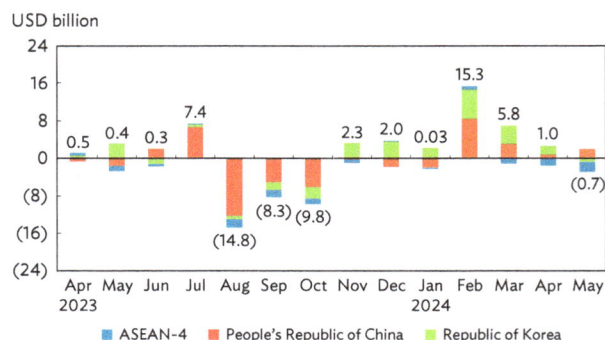

( ) = negative, USD = United States dollar.

Notes:
1. Data coverage is from 1 April 2023 to 31 May 2024.
2. The numbers above (below) each bar refer to net inflows (net outflows) for each month.
3. Emerging East Asia is defined to include member states of the Association of Southeast Asian Nations (ASEAN) plus the People's Republic of China; Hong Kong, China; and the Republic of Korea.
4. ASEAN-4 includes Indonesia, the Philippines, Thailand, and Viet Nam.

Source: Institute of International Finance.

During the review period, regional equity markets recorded mixed performances and posted aggregate portfolio inflows, mainly driven by domestic factors (**Figure F**). Regional equity markets rose an average of 0.9% (simple) and 2.9% (market-weighted), supported by the continued strong economic outlook.[3] The region's equity markets also received USD6.2 billion net inflows during the review period, buoyed by strong inflows in the Republic of Korea and the PRC (**Figure G**). In the Republic of Korea, capital inflows were supported by strong electronic chip demand amid an expected boom in interest in artificial intelligence. In the PRC, investors were encouraged by government efforts to support the stock market such as a plan to eliminate the dividend tax on stocks purchased through Stock Connect as well as the release of a capital reform plan by the State Council, which called for increasing dividend payments, enhancing the security of quantitative funds and strengthening corporate governance. However, ASEAN equity markets in the region recorded outflows of USD4.7 billion during the period over the increased likelihood of higher-for-longer interest rates.

The risks highlighted in the March 2024 edition of the *Asia Bond Monitor* remain relevant, particularly regarding uncertainty surrounding the path of the Federal Reserve's

monetary policy adjustment. Regional interest rates may remain elevated, as the Federal Reserve extends its tight monetary policy to address inflationary pressures. Expected higher-for-longer interest rates in the US could heighten risk aversion among investors, contributing to capital outflows and currency depreciations in the region. Higher-for-longer interest rates in the region would also exacerbate the debt burdens of public and private sector borrowers with high leverage.

Furthermore, geopolitical risks and extreme weather events have added to the probability of persistent inflation, supporting the likelihood of higher-for-longer interest rates. Ongoing geopolitical and trade tensions have increased freight rates this year. The container freight index, which tracks the cost of shipping containers on major trade lanes from Shanghai, rose 53.8% between 1 March and 31 May—driven by a sharp uptick in May caused by port congestion; container shortages; a surge in electric vehicle shipments to South America ahead of tariffs to be imposed by Brazil and Mexico in July on electric vehicles from the PRC; as well as geopolitical instability, especially from conflict in the Red Sea (**Figure H**). In addition, rising trade tensions between the US and the PRC could hurt domestic and external demand, affecting their respective trading partners.

---

[3] Asian Development Bank. 2024. *Asian Development Outlook April 2024*. Manila.

Heightened trade and geopolitical tensions could also amplify supply chain disruptions and hinder the progress of disinflation in both advanced economies and emerging

Figure H: Shanghai Containerized Freight Index

Index

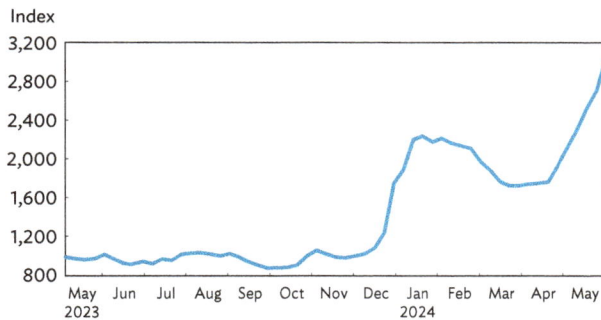

Notes:
1. Data are as of 31 May 2024.
2. The index reflects the spot rates of the Shanghai export container transport market. It includes both freight rates (indices) of 15 individual shipping routes and a composite index. Shipping routes are the major container trade routes of exports from Shanghai to the following regions: Europe; Mediterranean Sea; United States West Coast; United States East Coast; Persian Gulf; Australia and New Zealand; West Africa; South Africa; South America; West Japan; East Japan; Southeast Asia; Republic of Korea; Taipei,China; and Hong Kong, China.

Source: Based on Bloomberg LP data.

East Asia. Adverse weather patterns hold the potential to drive commodity prices higher. The extremely high temperatures and bad weather experienced across ASEAN economies during March–May contributed to the recent increase in food prices. With risks tilted to the downside, it is important to understand how adverse global shocks—including a longer-than-expected tight US monetary policy stance, elevated global financial market uncertainty, and global climate-related risks—could affect the transmission of monetary policy in emerging markets, as discussed in **Box 1**.

In the medium-term, addressing climate change is an important policy matter for the entire region. Financial markets should facilitate the mobilization of substantial climate-aligned investments. Aside from directing funding to green projects in the form of green finance, another important avenue would be to support the low-carbon transition of carbon assets. **Box 2** discusses how transition bonds enable carbon-intensive industries to enhance their environmental sustainability.

Box 1: Monetary Policy Transmission in Emerging Markets and the Role of Global Factors

There is growing evidence that macroeconomic conditions in emerging market economies (EMEs) have become more synchronized with global factors over the last 2 decades, as EMEs are increasingly integrated into the global economy through real and financial linkages (see, for example, De Leo, Gopinath, and Kalemli-Ozcan 2022; Miranda-Agrippino and Rey 2022).[a] New research by Renzhi and Beirne (2024) at the Asian Development Bank examines the extent to which the effectiveness of monetary policy in EMEs has been affected by global factors, including United States (US) monetary policy, global financial market uncertainty, and the impacts of climate change. Following the panel-local-projections framework proposed by Jordà (2005), Renzhi and Beirne (2024) estimate the impulse responses of key macroeconomic variables to monetary policy shocks in 24 EMEs from 2000 to 2022, conditioning on these global factors.[b]

To overcome potential endogeneity concerns, Renzhi and Beirne (2024) estimate a series of identified monetary policy shocks for each of the 24 EMEs. Using a set of structural vector autoregressive models, short-term interest rate changes are orthogonalized against the respective central bank's reactions to the macroeconomic environment, assuming a Taylor-type rule to determine the exogenous component. The estimated residuals can be considered exogenous monetary policy shocks and the source of the impulse response function analysis. The findings revealed that negative global shocks—including tightened US monetary policy, increased uncertainty in global financial markets, and the impacts of climate change—can weaken the transmission channels of monetary policy in EMEs. Specifically, industrial production and inflation are less affected by monetary policy shocks compared to when global factors are isolated. **Figure B1** presents the impacts of contractionary monetary policy shocks on industrial production and inflation, conditioned on the US monetary policy stance.[c]

---

[a] This box was written by John Beirne (principal economist) of the Asian Development Bank and Nuobu Renzhi (assistant professor) at the School of Economics of Capital University of Economics and Business in Beijing.
[b] The EMEs include Argentina; Brazil; Chile; Colombia; Czechia; Egypt; Hong Kong, China; Hungary; Indonesia; India; Israel; Mexico; Malaysia; the People's Republic of China; Peru; the Philippines; Poland; the Republic of Korea; Romania; the Russian Federation; Singapore; South Africa; Thailand; and Türkiye.
[c] Please refer to Renzhi and Beirne (2024) for the full set of results, including those that condition on global financial market uncertainty and climate change.

continued on next page

Box 1 *continued*

Figure B1: Impulse Responses to a Contractionary Monetary Policy Shock—United States Shadow Policy Rates

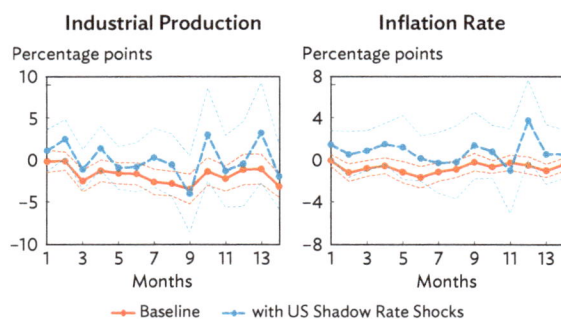

Industrial Production

Percentage points

Inflation Rate

Percentage points

— Baseline   — with US Shadow Rate Shocks

US = United States.

Notes: The figure plots the impulse responses of industrial production and inflation to a 100 basis points contractionary monetary policy shock, conditioned on US shadow policy rates. The dashed lines represent the 95% confidence bands. The US monetary policy stance is measured using the shadow policy rate proposed by Wu and Xia (2016), which reasonably reflects both conventional and unconventional monetary policy regimes.

Source: Renzhi, Nuobu, and John Beirne. 2024. Global Shocks and Monetary Policy Transmission in Emerging Markets. ADB Economics Working Paper No. 726; Wu, Jing C., and Fan Dora Xia. 2016. Measuring the Macroeconomic Impact of Monetary Policy at the Zero Lower Bound. *Journal of Money, Credit and Banking* 48 (2–3): 253–91.

The dashed blue lines in Figure B1 represent the estimated impulse responses in percentage points over the following 14 months to a contractionary monetary policy shock interacted with US shadow policy rates. By comparing to the baseline estimates that isolate the impacts of global factors (red solid line), the shocks that control for the US monetary policy stance seem to matter a great deal for monetary policy transmission in EMEs. Conditioned on the US shadow policy rate, unlike the baseline case, the response of industrial production is muted and not significantly different from zero, while the inflation rate exhibits little response. The results remain robust following a series of sensitivity checks that include alternative monetary policy measures.

Economy-specific characteristics across EMEs are also shown to affect monetary policy transmission from global shocks. Specifically, an enhanced degree of financial development can weaken the impacts of global shocks, while more capital account and trade openness can amplify these impacts. Deeper financial development may imply greater shock-absorbing capacity due to greater local market liquidity and financial intermediation efficiency. On the other hand, an economy with a higher degree of global financial integration is more likely to be exposed to external shocks through

temporary swings in capital flows, resulting in adverse macroeconomic outcomes.

The results have implications for EME monetary policies and central banks. It is important to build a sufficiently robust and flexible monetary policy operational framework that enables more resilience to external shocks. This can include bolstering the traditional monetary policy toolkit, such as targeted quantitative easing mechanisms. Through an extended toolkit in exceptional circumstances, the mandate of the central bank can be safeguarded while also limiting disruptions to the transmission of traditional monetary policy. Related to this, our findings provide a rationale for policymakers' use of other policy instruments in mitigating the adverse impacts of external shocks. This includes building up ample foreign exchange reserves, thereby enabling the central bank to intervene to mitigate the potential negative effects of global shocks on exchange rates and capital flows. In addition, policies such as macroprudential regulations that involve a broad range of measures aimed at buttressing financial stability could help to dampen the impacts of global financial shocks on economic activity in EMEs. Greater efforts to enhance the coordination of monetary and macroprudential policy, as well as fiscal policy, would also be useful measures.

References

De Leo, Pierre, Gita Gopinath, and Sebnem Kalemli-Ozcan. 2022. Monetary Policy Cyclicality in Emerging Economies. National Bureau of Economics Research Working Paper No. 30458.

Jordà, Oscar. 2005. Estimation and Inference of Impulse Responses by Local Projections. *American Economic Review* 95 (1): 161–82.

Miranda-Agrippino, Silvia, and Hélène Rey. 2022. The Global Financial Cycle. In *Handbook of International Economics, 6th Edition*, edited by Gita Gopinath, Elhanan Helpman, and Kenneth Rogoff, 1–43. Amsterdam: Elsevier.

Renzhi, Nuobu, and John Beirne. 2024. Global Shocks and Monetary Policy Transmission in Emerging Markets. ADB Economics Working Paper No. 726.

Wu, Jing C., and Fan Dora Xia. 2016. Measuring the Macroeconomic Impact of Monetary Policy at the Zero Lower Bound. *Journal of Money, Credit and Banking* 48 (2–3): 253–91.

Box 2: Promoting Transition Finance

Transition bonds refer to bonds that fund investments that are not necessarily green but result in reduced emissions from high-polluting economic sectors.[a] They currently represent less than 0.5% of the labeled bond market globally—with the most traction to date occurring in the People's Republic of China and Japan, as these two jurisdictions offer specific transition taxonomies. As of 2 April 2024, there were 73 transition bonds outstanding globally placed by 31 different issuers, of which 21 were entities from Japan (**Figure B2**).[b] The Government of Japan is the largest issuer of transition bonds with a 41% global market share.

Transition bonds are currently seen as an Asian-centric instrument and a large part of the growth in this market to date has been driven by official Japanese guidelines for transition bonds that have generated demand among both issuers and investors. Progress has also been made in accelerating the development of transition taxonomies and frameworks in the region via the latest Association of Southeast Asian Nations Taxonomy as well as ongoing efforts by the Hong Kong Monetary Authority. However, similar guidelines are presently lacking in other major economies outside of Asia.

Transition bonds are use-of-proceeds instruments designed to finance specific projects that reduce greenhouse gas emissions and/or support a company's progress toward its decarbonization goals. In contrast, the proceeds raised via sustainability-linked bonds can be used for general corporate purposes, provided it contributes to the bond's embedded long-term sustainability performance targets. In this respect, sustainability-linked bonds are performance-based instruments that allow issuers to commit explicitly to future improvements in sustainability outcomes.

Japan issued the world's first sovereign transition bond in the first quarter of 2024, raising JPY800 billion (USD5.3 billion) via a 10-year tenor. The issuance is part of a JPY20 trillion government program over the next 10 years. The Government of Japan's Climate Transition Bond Framework guided the eligible projects to be funded and received a Climate Bonds Initiative Certification, with second-party opinions provided by the Japan Credit Rating Agency and DNV Business Assurance Japan. The bond's structure was aligned with Japan's Basic Guidelines on Climate Transition Finance and Green Bond Guidelines, as well as the International Capital Market Association's Climate Transition Finance Handbook and Green Bond Principles. The issuance featured an additional layer of credibility as the bond is eligible for inclusion in international green bond funds and indices.

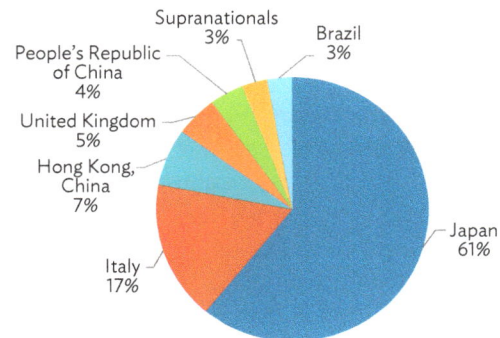

Figure B2: Global Transition Bonds Outstanding by Market (%)

Source: Environmental Finance Data (accessed on 2 April 2024).

Despite the very positive approach employed by the government—the deal was 2.9 times oversubscribed, a good but not exceptional result for a Japanese Government Bond auction—the 0.7% coupon was priced at a yield of 0.74%, or 1 basis point (bp) inside where the 10-year Japanese Government Bond was trading. Thus, the "greenium" of 1 bp was smaller than the 2–3 bps greenium usually achieved by Japanese local government issuers of green and social bonds, suggesting that international investor demand for these instruments still has some way to go.

There is anecdotal evidence that the transition bond market is expanding and internationalizing. The Italian utilities provider Snam is now the second-largest transition bond issuer globally, having raised a total of USD4.3 billion from eight issues with tenors of 4–10 years. Snam's green finance framework referenced the International Capital Market Association's Green Bond Principles as supportive standards and is aligned with the European Union's Taxonomy.

Clearly, there is an urgent need for a common global approach to help create a more harmonized transition finance landscape, building on the progress already achieved in Asia. Otherwise, there is a risk of creating a fragmented regulatory landscape for transition bonds reflecting the peculiarities of each jurisdiction. The key to the ongoing success of green and sustainable bond markets is a well-established global standard—be it in use of proceeds or a sustainability-linked format. It is crucial to build the same traction in the transition bond market.

---

[a] This box was written by Jim Turnbull, deputy director and head of product of the Capital and Financial Markets Development Group at the European Bank for Reconstruction and Development, and Razvan Dumitrescu, head of sustainable finance at Emirates NBD Capital.
[b] Environmental Finance Data (accessed on 2 April 2024).

Bond Market Developments in the First Quarter of 2024

Section 1. Local Currency Bonds Outstanding

Emerging East Asian local currency (LCY) bonds outstanding rose to USD24.7 trillion at the end of March on a year-on-year (y-o-y) expansion of 8.9%.[4] The pace of annual growth in emerging East Asian LCY bonds outstanding continued to surpass that of the United States (US) (7.8%) and the European Union 20 (EU-20) (6.1%). At the end of March, the market size of emerging East Asian LCY bonds was equivalent to 64.0% of the US bond market (USD38.6 trillion) and 115.3% of the EU-20 (USD21.4 trillion) (**Figure 1**).

Figure 1: Local Currency Bonds Outstanding in Emerging East Asia, the European Union 20, and the United States

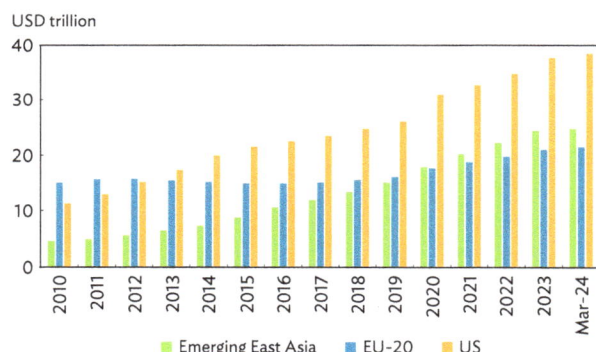

USD trillion

EU-20 = European Union 20, US = United States, USD = United States dollar.

Notes:
1. Emerging East Asia is defined to include the Association of Southeast Asian Nations plus the People's Republic of China; Hong Kong, China; and the Republic of Korea.
2. The EU-20 includes the member markets of Austria, Belgium, Croatia, Cyprus, Estonia, Finland, France, Germany, Greece, Ireland, Italy, Latvia, Lithuania, Luxembourg, Malta, the Netherlands, Portugal, Slovakia, Slovenia, and Spain.

Sources: People's Republic of China (CEIC Data Company); Hong Kong, China (Hong Kong Monetary Authority); EU-20 (European Central Bank); Indonesia (Bank Indonesia; Directorate General of Budget Financing and Risk Management, Ministry of Finance; and Indonesia Stock Exchange); Republic of Korea (Bank of Korea and KG Zeroin Corporation); Malaysia (Bank Negara Malaysia); Philippines (Bureau of the Treasury and Bloomberg LP); Singapore (Monetary Authority of Singapore and Bloomberg LP); Thailand (Bank of Thailand); United States (Securities Industry and Financial Markets Association and Bloomberg LP); and Viet Nam (Vietnam Bond Market Association and Bloomberg LP).

Quarterly growth in the emerging East Asian LCY bond market in the first quarter (Q1) of 2024 was down from the previous quarter, largely due to a contraction of Treasury issuance in the People's Republic of China (PRC). The region's LCY bonds outstanding rose 1.4% quarter-on-quarter (q-o-q) in Q1 2024, down from 1.8% q-o-q growth in the fourth quarter (Q4) of 2023 (**Table 1**). Growth in the region's Treasury bonds outstanding eased to 1.3% q-o-q in Q1 2024 from 5.0% q-o-q in Q4 2023, mostly due to a deeper contraction in Treasury bond issuance in the PRC and Hong Kong, China. All other emerging East Asian economies saw increased issuance of Treasury bonds. The region's corporate bond market expanded 1.2% q-o-q in Q1 2024, recovering from a contraction of 3.3% q-o-q in Q4 2023 and supported by increased issuance in the PRC; Hong Kong, China; and Singapore. All regional bond markets posted positive quarterly growth in Q1 2024, with Thailand and Viet Nam recovering from contractions in the preceding quarter (**Figure 2**).

The amount of LCY bonds outstanding in the Association of Southeast Asian Nations (ASEAN) members remains relatively small compared to other emerging East Asian economies. ASEAN LCY bonds outstanding reached USD2.2 trillion at the end of March, representing 8.9% of the emerging East Asian LCY bond market. During the same period, the PRC's LCY bond market (USD19.7 trillion) accounted for 79.7% of the region's total, followed by the Republic of Korea (USD2.4 trillion) at 9.8% (**Figure 3**). Treasury bonds (USD15.3 trillion) accounted for 62.0% of the emerging East Asian LCY bond market at the end of March, while corporate bonds (USD8.8 trillion) and central bank bonds (USD0.6 trillion) comprised the remaining 35.5% and 2.4%, respectively.

A majority of LCY Treasury bonds outstanding in ASEAN economies at the end of Q1 2024 were medium- to long-term tenor bonds. At the end of March, around 52.6% of outstanding Treasury bonds in

---

4 Emerging East Asia is defined to include member states of the Association of Southeast Asian Nations (ASEAN) plus the People's Republic of China; Hong Kong, China; and the Republic of Korea.

Table 1: Size and Composition of Select Emerging East Asian Local Currency Bond Markets

	Q1 2023		Q4 2023		Q1 2024			Growth Rate (%) Q1 2024	
	Amount (USD billion)	% of GDP	Amount (USD billion)	% of GDP	Amount (USD billion)	% share	% of GDP	q-o-q	y-o-y
People's Republic of China									
Total	18,957	106.9	19,769	111.3	19,667	100.0	111.6	1.2	9.0
Treasury and Other Government	12,489	70.4	13,096	73.7	13,031	66.3	74.0	1.2	9.6
Central Bank	2	0.01	2	0.01	2	0.01	0.01	0.0	0.0
Corporate	6,465	36.4	6,671	37.6	6,634	33.7	37.7	1.2	7.8
Hong Kong, China									
Total	358	98.8	388	101.5	389	100.0	100.4	0.6	8.4
Treasury and Other Government	29	8.0	36	9.5	37	9.4	9.5	0.9	26.6
Government	155	42.8	161	42.1	162	41.7	41.8	1.0	4.2
Corporate	174	48.0	190	49.9	190	48.9	49.1	0.1	9.1
Indonesia									
Total	411	30.6	428	31.5	428	100.0	32.1	3.1	10.2
Treasury and Other Government	377	28.1	377	27.8	370	86.5	27.8	1.1	3.8
Central Bank	4	0.3	21	1.5	29	6.7	2.2	43.0	730.0
Corporate	30	2.2	30	2.2	29	6.8	2.2	(0.2)	2.5
Republic of Korea									
Total	2,315	152.8	2,497	161.2	2,426	100.0	162.5	1.6	8.5
Treasury and Other Government	892	58.9	933	60.2	906	37.4	60.7	1.6	5.1
Central Bank	94	6.2	94	6.1	89	3.7	2.1	(1.4)	(1.8)
Corporate	1,329	87.7	1,470	94.9	1,431	59.0	95.9	1.8	11.4
Malaysia									
Total	433	124.8	437	128.0	432	100.0	128.8	1.7	6.6
Treasury and Other Government	247	71.1	249	72.9	250	57.8	74.4	3.2	8.1
Central Bank	0.5	0.1	4	1.1	3	0.6	0.8	(24.4)	550.0
Corporate	186	53.5	184	54.0	180	41.6	53.6	0.2	3.4
Philippines									
Total	212	50.8	217	49.4	219	100.0	49.6	2.2	6.4
Treasury and Other Government	173	41.5	178	40.6	180	82.5	40.9	2.7	7.6
Central Bank	10	2.4	11	2.6	14	6.2	3.1	20.2	37.5
Corporate	29	6.9	27	6.2	25	11.3	5.6	(8.2)	(11.7)
Singapore									
Total	502	97.7	542	106.3	545	100.0	107.4	2.7	10.0
Treasury and Other Government	175	34.0	195	38.2	192	35.3	37.9	1.0	11.6
Central Bank	195	37.9	223	43.6	228	41.9	45.0	4.7	18.8
Corporate	132	25.8	125	24.5	124	22.8	24.5	1.6	(4.9)
Thailand									
Total	466	90.6	483	92.0	465	100.0	94.0	2.8	6.2
Treasury and Other Government	264	51.2	276	52.5	269	57.7	54.3	3.9	8.5
Central Bank	68	13.2	65	12.4	65	13.9	13.1	5.7	1.1
Corporate	135	26.2	142	27.0	132	28.3	26.6	(0.9)	4.3
Viet Nam									
Total	113	27.3	109	26.0	115	100.0	27.4	7.7	8.2
Treasury and Other Government	77	18.5	80	19.0	81	70.1	19.2	3.3	11.6
Central Bank	5	1.1	0	0.0	6	5.1	1.4	–	32.1
Corporate	31	7.6	29	7.0	29	24.8	6.8	(0.9)	(3.7)
Emerging East Asia									
Total	23,767	102.6	24,871	106.8	24,687	100.0	107.2	1.4	8.9
Treasury and Other Government	14,723	63.5	15,420	66.2	15,317	62.0	66.5	1.3	9.2
Central Bank	533	2.3	581	2.5	597	2.4	2.6	5.3	14.3
Corporate	8,511	36.7	8,870	38.1	8,773	35.5	38.1	1.2	7.9
Japan									
Total	10,184	238.7	9,670	230.5	9,078	100.0	230.3	0.7	1.5
Treasury and Other Government	9,409	220.6	8,918	212.6	8,376	92.3	212.5	0.8	1.4
Central Bank	33	0.8	27	0.6	25	0.3	0.6	(1.5)	(14.3)
Corporate	742	17.4	725	17.3	677	7.5	17.2	0.3	3.9

( ) = negative, – = not applicable, GDP = gross domestic product, q-o-q = quarter-on-quarter, Q1 = first quarter, Q4 = fourth quarter, USD = United States dollar, y-o-y = year-on-year.

Notes:
1. For Singapore, corporate bonds outstanding are based on *AsianBondsOnline* estimates.
2. Data for GDP is from CEIC Data Company.
3. Bloomberg LP end-of-period local currency–USD rates are used.
4. Growth rates are calculated from a local currency base and do not include currency effects. For emerging East Asia, growth figures are based on 31 March 2024 currency exchange rates and do not include currency effects.

Sources: People's Republic of China (CEIC Data Company); Hong Kong, China (Hong Kong Monetary Authority); Indonesia (Bank Indonesia; Directorate General of Budget Financing and Risk Management, Ministry of Finance; and Indonesia Stock Exchange); Japan (Japan Securities Dealers Association); Republic of Korea (Bank of Korea and KG Zeroin Corporation); Malaysia (Bank Negara Malaysia); Philippines (Bureau of the Treasury and Bloomberg LP); Singapore (Monetary Authority of Singapore and Bloomberg LP); Thailand (Bank of Thailand); and Viet Nam (Vietnam Bond Market Association and Bloomberg LP).

Figure 2: Growth of Select Emerging East Asian Local Currency Bond Markets (q-o-q, %)

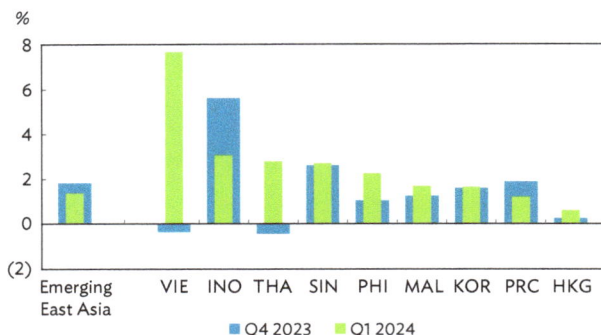

( ) = negative; HKG = Hong Kong, China; INO = Indonesia; KOR = Republic of Korea; MAL = Malaysia; PHI = Philippines; PRC = People's Republic of China; Q1 = first quarter; Q4 = fourth quarter; q-o-q = quarter-on-quarter; SIN = Singapore; THA = Thailand; VIE = Viet Nam.

Notes:
1. For Singapore, corporate bonds outstanding are based on *AsianBondsOnline* estimates.
2. Growth rates are calculated from a local currency base and do not include currency effects. For emerging East Asia, growth figures are based on 31 March 2024 currency exchange rates and do not include currency effects.

Sources: People's Republic of China (CEIC Data Company); Hong Kong, China (Hong Kong Monetary Authority); Indonesia (Bank Indonesia; Directorate General of Budget Financing and Risk Management, Ministry of Finance; and Indonesia Stock Exchange); Republic of Korea (Bank of Korea and KG Zeroin Corporation); Malaysia (Bank Negara Malaysia); Philippines (Bureau of the Treasury and Bloomberg LP); Singapore (Monetary Authority of Singapore and Bloomberg LP); Thailand (Bank of Thailand); and Viet Nam (Vietnam Bond Market Association and Bloomberg LP).

Figure 3: Local Currency Bonds Outstanding in Emerging East Asia by Economy and Type of Bond as of 31 March 2024

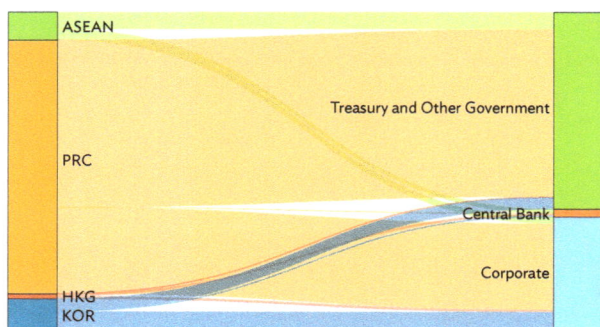

ASEAN = Association of Southeast Asian Nations; HKG = Hong Kong, China; KOR = Republic of Korea; PRC = People's Republic of China.

Note: ASEAN comprises the markets of Indonesia, Malaysia, the Philippines, Singapore, Thailand, and Viet Nam.

Source: *AsianBondsOnline* calculations based on various local sources.

Figure 4: Maturity Structure of Local Currency Treasury Bonds Outstanding in Select Emerging East Asian Markets as of 31 March 2024

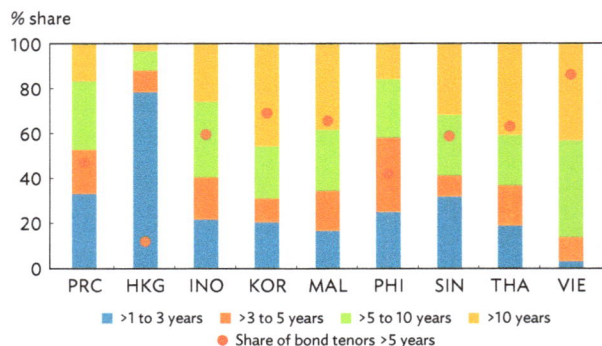

HKG = Hong Kong, China; INO = Indonesia; KOR = Republic of Korea; MAL = Malaysia; PHI = Philippines; PRC = People's Republic of China; SIN = Singapore; THA = Thailand; VIE = Viet Nam.

Note: Treasury bonds are local-currency-denominated, fixed-income securities issued by a government with maturities longer than 1 year.

Sources: People's Republic of China (Bloomberg LP); Hong Kong, China (Hong Kong Monetary Authority); Indonesia (Directorate General of Budget Financing and Risk Management, Ministry of Finance); Republic of Korea (Bloomberg LP); Malaysia (Bank Negara Malaysia Fully Automated System for Issuing/Tendering); Philippines (Bureau of the Treasury); Singapore (Monetary Authority of Singapore); Thailand (Bank of Thailand); and Viet Nam (Bloomberg LP).

emerging East Asia had maturities of over 5 years. This share was even higher in ASEAN markets (60.4%), with Viet Nam and Malaysia having the region's highest shares at 86.2% and 65.6%, respectively (**Figure 4**). The size-weighted average tenor of Treasury bonds outstanding was 8.2 years for all emerging East Asian markets and 8.3 years for ASEAN markets. These averages exceed the US average (7.8 years) but are lower than the EU-20's (8.6 years). The LCY bond market in Hong Kong, China has a relatively large share of shorter-term Treasury bonds, with 88.1% of outstanding Treasury bonds carrying maturities of 5 years or below.

LCY Treasury bonds in emerging East Asia remained largely held by passive investor groups, with some regional markets witnessing improved investor diversity in Q1 2024. Banking institutions were the largest Treasury bond holders in the region, accounting for 36.6% of Treasury bonds outstanding at the end of March. The share of bank holdings was highest in the PRC (70.0%), followed by the Philippines (46.9%) (**Figure 5**). The region's next largest investor group comprised insurance and pension funds (28.9%), whose holdings were the highest in Viet Nam 60.8%), Thailand (43.1%), and

Figure 5: Investor Profiles of Local Currency Treasury Bonds in Select Emerging East Asian Markets

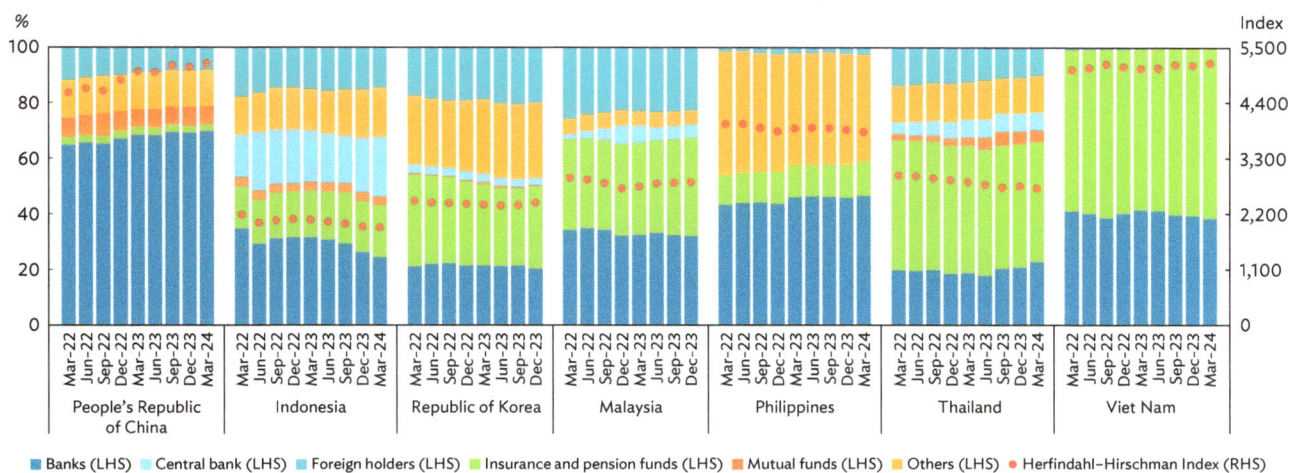

LHS = left-hand side, RHS = right-hand side.
Notes:
1. Data for the Republic of Korea and Malaysia are up to December 2023.
2. "Others" include government institutions, individuals, securities companies, custodians, private corporations, and all other investors not elsewhere classified.
3. The Herfindahl–Hirschman Index is a commonly accepted measure of market concentration. In this case, the index was used to measure the investor profile diversification of the local currency bond markets and is calculated by summing the squared share of each investor group in the bond market.

Sources: People's Republic of China (CEIC Data Company); Indonesia (Directorate General of Budget Financing and Risk Management, Ministry of Finance); Republic of Korea (Bank of Korea); Malaysia (Bank Negara Malaysia); Philippines (Bureau of the Treasury); Thailand (Bank of Thailand); and Viet Nam (Ministry of Finance).

Malaysia (35.2%). Across the region, Indonesia and the Republic of Korea have the most diversified investor bases, as reflected in their low Herfindahl–Hirschman Index scores, while the PRC and Viet Nam have the most concentrated investor profiles.[5] In Viet Nam, two major investor groups—banks and insurance and pension funds—collectively held 99.5% of outstanding Treasury bonds at the end of March. During Q1 2024, Indonesia, the Philippines, and Thailand showed slight declines in their respective Herfindahl–Hirschman Index scores, reflecting improvement in investor base diversity.

Section 2. Local Currency Bond Issuance

LCY bond issuance in emerging East Asia fell 9.0% q-o-q in Q1 2024 as both government and corporate bond issuance contracted on segment-specific factors. Total regional LCY bond issuance reached USD2.2 trillion in Q1 2024, less than half that in the US (USD5.1 trillion) but almost double that in the EU-20 (USD1.2 trillion). Six out of nine economies in the region registered reduced issuance in Q1 2024

compared with Q4 2023. The contraction in regional government bonds was driven by reduced issuance in the PRC, due to a higher issuance base in Q4 2023 when some 2024 financing quotas were frontloaded, which more than offset rising government bond issuance in the Republic of Korea and all ASEAN markets during Q1 2024. In the corporate bond segment, the Republic of Korea and almost all ASEAN economies witnessed declining issuance in Q1 2024 due to higher-for-longer interest rates resulting from the delayed US rate cut. Meanwhile, corporate bond issuance in the PRC increased in Q1 2024 due to lower bond yields, driven by the People's Bank of China's monetary easing (**Figure 6**).

Government bond issuance decreased 18.1% q-o-q to USD853.8 billion in Q1 2024, dragged down by the contraction in the PRC. The PRC, which accounted for 82.3% of regional government issuance during the quarter, registered a contraction in government bond issuance of 24.4% q-o-q in Q1 2024 (**Figure 7**). This contraction was mostly due to a high base effect from Q4 2023, when local governments frontloaded part of their respective 2024 issuance quotas. ASEAN markets collectively

[5] The Herfindahl–Hirschman Index is a commonly accepted measure of market concentration. The index is used to measure the investor profile diversification of the region's local currency bond markets and is calculated by summing the squared share of each investor group in the bond market.

Figure 6: Local Currency Bond Issuance in Select Emerging East Asian Markets

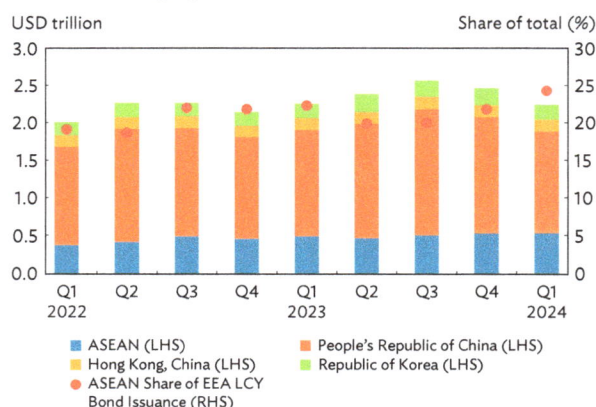

ASEAN = Association of Southeast Asian Nations, EEA = emerging East Asia, LCY = local currency, LHS = left-hand side, Q1 = first quarter, Q2 = second quarter, Q3 = third quarter, Q4 = fourth quarter, RHS = right-hand side, USD = United States dollar.

Notes:
1. ASEAN comprises the markets of Indonesia, Malaysia, the Philippines, Singapore, Thailand, and Viet Nam.
2. Figures were computed based on 31 March 2024 currency exchange rates and do not include currency effects.

Source: People's Republic of China (CEIC Data Company); Hong Kong, China (Hong Kong Monetary Authority); Indonesia (Bank Indonesia; Directorate General of Budget Financing and Risk Management, Ministry of Finance; and Indonesia Stock Exchange); Republic of Korea (Bank of Korea and KG Zeroin Corporation); Malaysia (Bank Negara Malaysia); Philippines (Bureau of the Treasury and Bloomberg LP); Singapore (Monetary Authority of Singapore and Bloomberg LP); Thailand (Bank of Thailand and Thai Bond Market Association); and Viet Nam (Viet Nam Bond Market Association and Bloomberg LP).

Figure 7: Local Currency Bond Issuance in Emerging East Asia by Economy and Type of Bond in the First Quarter of 2024

ASEAN = Association of Southeast Asian Nations; HKG = Hong Kong, China; KOR = Republic of Korea; PRC = People's Republic of China.

Note: ASEAN comprises the markets of Indonesia, Malaysia, the Philippines, Singapore, Thailand, and Viet Nam.

Source: *AsianBondsOnline* calculations based on various local sources.

accounted for 12.5% of the regional government issuance total in Q1 2024, posting a significant increase of 38.9% q-o-q. This was due to the large volume of issuance in the Philippines—where PHP584.9 billion (USD10.4 billion) of Retail Treasury Bonds were issued in February to fund programs in key sectors of the economy—and a result of frontloading issuance policies in some ASEAN markets. In the Republic of Korea, issuance grew 39.6% q-o-q as the government planned to spend more than 65% of its fiscal budget in the first half of the year. Meanwhile, issuance of central bank bonds in the region contracted 2.8% q-o-q in Q1 2024, with ASEAN markets accounting for almost 75% of the regional central bank total.

Corporate bond issuance contracted 1.9% q-o-q in Q1 2024 to USD822.1 billion on higher-for-longer interest rates. Corporate bond issuance in the PRC, which accounted for 76.9% of the regional total in Q1 2024, increased 3.8% q-o-q, reversing the 12.6% q-o-q contraction in Q4 2023 (**Table 2**). The rebound was supported by the decline in domestic bond yields, spurred by the People's Bank of China's monetary easing to support economic activities. In contrast, almost all other regional markets recorded lower corporate bond issuance in Q1 2024 compared to Q4 2023 due to rising bond yields on the expectation of higher-for-longer interest rates in the US. The Republic of Korea and ASEAN markets, which accounted for 16.0% and 3.1% of the regional corporate issuance total, respectively, posted 24.4% q-o-q and 18.4% q-o-q contractions in Q1 2024.

Around 54.7% of regional Treasury bond issuance in Q1 2024 carried medium- to long-term tenors (**Figure 8a**). The trend toward longer tenors was most evident in the Republic of Korea and a majority of ASEAN economies (**Figure 8b**). The size-weighted average maturity of regional Treasury bond issuance inched up to 7.7 years in Q1 2024 from 7.3 years in Q4 2023, with ASEAN economies and the Republic of Korea recording averages of 9.9 years and 17.4 years, respectively. Meanwhile, over half of Hong Kong, China's Treasury bond issuance was concentrated in shorter tenors of 3 years or less, as these bonds are mostly used to provide benchmark rates and help develop the domestic bond market.

Table 2: Local-Currency-Denominated Bond Issuance

	Q1 2023		Q4 2023		Q1 2024		Growth Rate (%)	
	Amount (USD billion)	% share	Amount (USD billion)	% share	Amount (USD billion)	% share	Q1 2024	
							q-o-q	y-o-y
People's Republic of China								
Total	1,475	100.0	1,565	100.0	1,335	100.0	(13.3)	(4.9)
Treasury and Other Government	860	58.3	946	60.4	703	52.7	(24.4)	(14.1)
Central Bank	0	0.0	0	0.0	0	0.0	–	–
Corporate	615	41.7	619	39.6	632	47.3	3.8	8.0
Hong Kong, China								
Total	161	100.0	158	100.0	162	100.0	2.9	0.6
Treasury and Other Government	1	0.6	4	2.5	0.7	0.4	(82.0)	(29.5)
Government	124	77.3	129	81.9	128	79.1	(0.6)	2.9
Corporate	35	22.0	25	15.6	33	20.5	34.8	(6.6)
Indonesia								
Total	36	100.0	44	100.0	43	100.0	(0.6)	24.5
Treasury and Other Government	16	45.1	11	25.5	16	37.6	46.8	3.8
Central Bank	18	49.8	31	69.0	25	58.6	(15.6)	46.4
Corporate	2	5.0	2	5.5	2	3.8	(31.9)	(7.3)
Republic of Korea								
Total	190	100.0	232	100.0	193	100.0	(13.0)	5.1
Treasury and Other Government	44	23.0	32	14.0	43	22.4	39.6	2.3
Central Bank	26	13.5	17	7.5	18	9.3	7.8	(27.7)
Corporate	120	63.4	182	78.5	132	68.2	(24.4)	13.1
Malaysia								
Total	23	100.0	34	100.0	29	100.0	(12.8)	31.8
Treasury and Other Government	16	68.0	10	29.1	11	37.1	11.1	(28.1)
Central Bank	0.5	2.0	14	41.4	10	36.4	(23.4)	2,350.0
Corporate	7	30.0	10	29.4	8	26.5	(21.5)	16.3
Philippines								
Total	50	100.0	41	100.0	56	100.0	37.3	16.0
Treasury and Other Government	17	34.8	8	19.0	22	39.9	188.6	33.1
Central Bank	32	64.2	32	77.8	32	57.8	2.0	4.4
Corporate	0.5	1.0	1	3.2	1	2.3	(0.1)	163.7
Singapore								
Total	295	100.0	352	100.0	340	100.0	(1.1)	16.9
Treasury and Other Government	29	9.9	35	9.8	37	10.7	8.0	26.3
Central Bank	264	89.4	316	89.8	301	88.4	(2.6)	15.7
Corporate	2	0.7	1	0.4	3	0.9	103.6	38.2
Thailand								
Total	73	100.0	58	100.0	61	100.0	12.2	(11.0)
Treasury and Other Government	23	31.6	14	24.7	18	29.4	33.9	(17.0)
Central Bank	34	46.5	30	52.2	32	52.1	11.9	(0.2)
Corporate	16	21.9	13	23.1	11	18.5	(10.3)	(24.9)
Viet Nam								
Total	41	100.0	17	100.0	10	100.0	(36.7)	(73.4)
Treasury and Other Government	6	14.5	2	10.2	4	35.6	120.1	(34.5)
Central Bank	34	82.5	11	66.4	6	57.5	(45.2)	(81.5)
Corporate	1	3.0	4	23.4	0.7	6.9	(81.3)	(38.5)
Emerging East Asia								
Total	2,343	100.0	2,500	100.0	2,228	100.0	(9.0)	(1.0)
Treasury and Other Government	1,012	43.2	1,062	42.5	854	38.3	(18.1)	(11.5)
Central Bank	532	22.7	580	23.2	553	24.8	(2.8)	5.9
Corporate	800	34.1	858	34.3	822	36.9	(1.9)	7.6
Japan								
Total	489	100.0	431	100.0	371	100.0	(7.7)	(13.6)
Treasury and Other Government	466	95.2	389	90.2	351	94.6	(3.2)	(14.2)
Central Bank	0	0.0	14	3.3	0	0.0	(100.0)	–
Corporate	23	4.8	28	6.5	20	5.4	(23.6)	(1.7)

( ) = negative, – = not applicable, Q1 = first quarter, Q4 = fourth quarter, q-o-q = quarter-on-quarter, USD = United States dollar, y-o-y = year-on-year.

Notes:
1. Data reflect gross bond issuance.
2. Bloomberg LP end-of-period local currency–USD rates are used.
3. Growth rates are calculated from a local currency base and do not include currency effects. For emerging East Asia, growth figures are based on 31 March 2024 currency exchange rates and do not include currency effects.

Source: People's Republic of China (CEIC Data Company); Hong Kong, China (Hong Kong Monetary Authority); Indonesia (Bank Indonesia, Directorate General of Budget Financing and Risk Management, Ministry of Finance; and Indonesia Stock Exchange); Japan (Japan Securities Dealers Association); Republic of Korea (Bank of Korea and KG Zeroin Corporation); Malaysia (Bank Negara Malaysia); Philippines (Bureau of the Treasury and Bloomberg LP); Singapore (Monetary Authority of Singapore and Bloomberg LP); Thailand (Bank of Thailand and Thai Bond Market Association); and Viet Nam (Vietnam Bond Market Association and Bloomberg LP).

Figure 8: Maturity Structure of Local Currency Treasury Bond Issuance in Emerging East Asia

a. Quarterly Maturity Structure

b. Maturity Structure by Market, Q1 2024

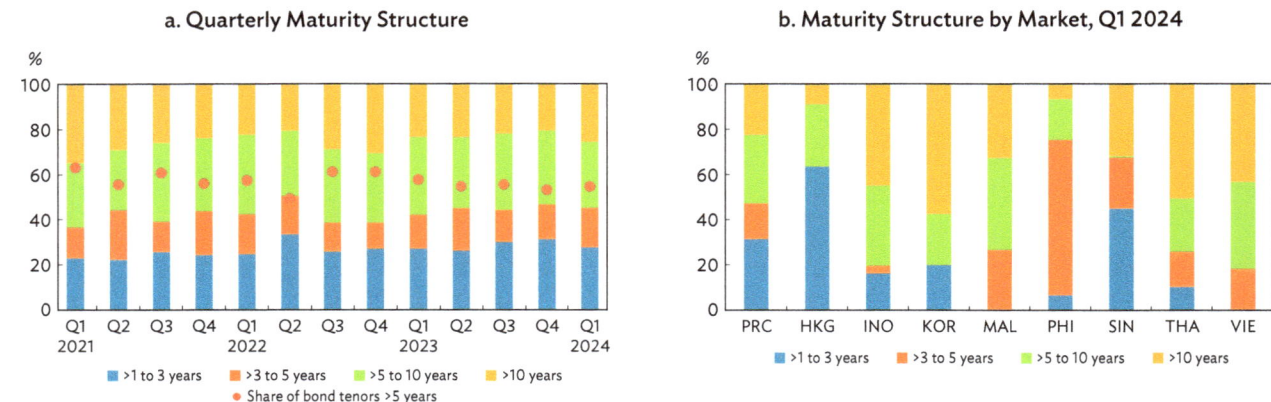

HKG = Hong Kong, China; INO = Indonesia; KOR = Republic of Korea; MAL = Malaysia; PHI = Philippines; PRC = People's Republic of China; Q1 = first quarter; Q2 = second quarter; Q3 = third quarter; Q4 = fourth quarter; SIN = Singapore; THA = Thailand; VIE = Viet Nam.

Notes:
1. Figures were computed based on 31 March 2024 currency exchange rates and do not include currency effects.
2. Treasury bonds are local-currency-denominated, fixed-income securities issued by a government with maturities longer than 1 year.

Source: *AsianBondsOnline* calculations based on various local sources.

Section 3. Intra-Regional Bond Issuance

Emerging East Asia's intra-regional bond issuance contracted amid the high interest rate environment.
Intra-regional bond issuance in emerging East Asia recorded USD8.9 billion in Q1 2024, down 3.9% q-o-q from USD9.2 billion in Q4 2023 (**Figure 9**).[6] Only three markets issued intra-regional bonds during Q1 2024, compared to five in the prior quarter. The significant decline of intra-regional bond issuance from the Republic of Korea dragged down the region's total issuance, offsetting increased issuance in Q1 2024 from Hong Kong, China and Singapore. The Republic of Korea's issuance declined 44.8% q-o-q to USD0.3 billion, accounting for only 3.1% of the regional total and down from USD0.5 billion in Q4 2023. Hong Kong, China remained the largest issuer of intra-regional bonds in emerging East Asia, accounting for 91.1% of the region's total. Hong Kong, China's total issuance reached USD8.1 billion in Q1 2024, an increase of 3.5% q-o-q from USD7.8 billion in the previous quarter. Singapore's issuance increased 4.2% q-o-q to USD0.5 billion in Q1 2024, equivalent to 5.8% of total intra-regional issuance. Among corporate issuers of intra-regional bonds in emerging East Asia, China Merchants Group—a state-owned logistics company domiciled in Hong Kong, China—

Figure 9: Intra-Regional Bond Issuance in Select Emerging East Asian Economies

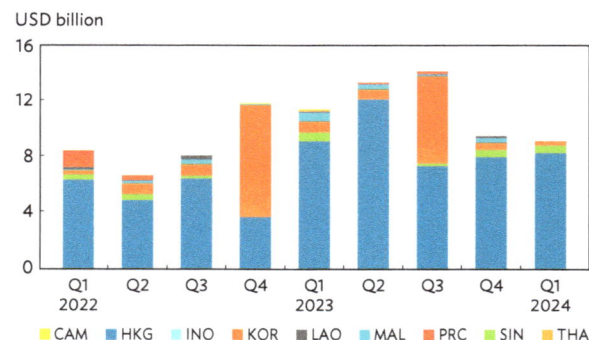

CAM = Cambodia; HKG = Hong Kong, China; INO = Indonesia; KOR = Republic of Korea; LAO = Lao People's Democratic Republic; MAL = Malaysia; PRC = People's Republic of China; Q1 = first quarter; Q2 = second quarter; Q3 = third quarter; Q4 = fourth quarter; SIN = Singapore; THA = Thailand; USD = United States dollar.

Notes:
1. Emerging East Asia is defined to include member states of the Association of Southeast Asian Nations (ASEAN) plus the People's Republic of China; Hong Kong, China; and the Republic of Korea.
2. Intra-regional bond issuance is defined as emerging East Asian bond issuance denominated in a regional currency excluding the issuer's home currency.
3. Figures were computed based on 31 March 2024 currency exchange rates and do not include currency effects.

Source: *AsianBondsOnline* calculations based on Bloomberg LP data.

remained the largest issuer during the quarter with aggregate issuance of USD3.1 billion, accounting for 38.9% of the regional total.

---

[6] Intra-regional bond issuance is defined as emerging East Asian bond issuance denominated in a regional currency excluding the issuer's home currency.

The transportation sector dominated intra-regional bond issuance in Q1 2024, and the Chinese yuan remained the prevalent issuing currency in the region. CNY-denominated issuance accounted for 96.9% of emerging East Asia's intra-regional total, reaching a total of USD8.6 billion during the quarter (**Figure 10**). CNY-denominated issuance came from Hong Kong, China and Singapore, while HKD-denominated issuance came from the Republic of Korea and Singapore. The Republic of Korea was the only source of SGD-denominated intra-regional bonds in Q1 2024. Collectively, issuances denominated in Hong Kong dollars and Singapore dollars accounted for 3.1% of the total intra-regional issuance in the region. By sector, issuance from the transportation industry totaled USD3.5 billion in Q1 2024, up 18.2% q-o-q from the previous quarter's USD3.0 billion. Intra-regional issuance from the transportation sector comprised 39.2% of the regional total in Q1 2024, while financial sector issuance totaled USD3.3 billion and accounted for 37.1% of the regional total. Issuance from the utilities and real estate sectors decreased on a q-o-q basis during Q1 2024, accounting for 10.4% and 6.4%, respectively, of emerging East Asia's total intra-regional bond issuance.

Section 4. G3 Currency Bond Issuance

Quarterly growth in G3 currency bond issuance in emerging East Asia picked up in Q1 2024 on increased issuance across most markets in the region.[7] G3 currency bond issuance recorded USD50.1 billion in Q1 2024, increasing 11.0% q-o-q and exceeding the expansion of 9.4% q-o-q in the previous quarter, as most regional economies increased their G3 bond issuance during the review period (**Figure 11**). On a y-o-y basis, however, G3 currency bond issuance during the quarter was 14.2% lower as issuance of USD- and EUR-denominated bonds, which constituted 93.5% and 4.7% of the regional total, respectively, both fell amid higher interest rates in the US and the euro area. During the review period, the Republic of Korea overtook the PRC as the top issuer in the region with USD14.7 billion raised in G3 currency bonds, while the PRC raised USD14.2 billion. G3 currency bonds issued in the ASEAN region totaled USD15.3 billion, representing 30.6% of emerging East Asia's issuance total in Q1 2024 (**Figure 12**). ASEAN's G3 bond issuance increased 51.8% q-o-q and 34.4% y-o-y. Indonesia and Malaysia led all ASEAN economies in G3 currency bond issuance

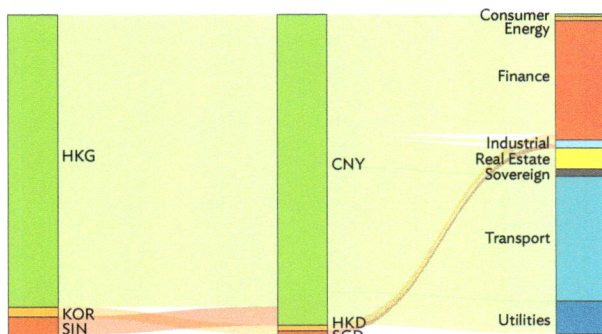

Figure 10: Intra-Regional Bond Issuance in Emerging East Asia by Economy, Currency, and Sector in the First Quarter of 2024

CNY = Chinese yuan; HKD = Hong Kong dollar; HKG = Hong Kong, China; KOR = Republic of Korea; SGD = Singapore dollar; SIN = Singapore.

Note: Intra-regional bond issuance is defined as emerging East Asian bond issuance denominated in a regional currency excluding the issuer's home currency.

Source: *AsianBondsOnline* calculations based on Bloomberg LP data.

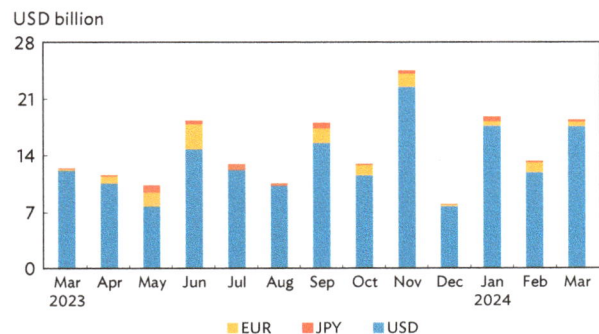

Figure 11: Monthly G3 Currency Bond Issuance in Select Emerging East Asian Markets

EUR = euro, JPY = Japanese yen, USD = United States dollar.

Notes:
1. Emerging East Asia is defined to include member states of the Association of Southeast Asian Nations plus the People's Republic of China; Hong Kong, China; and the Republic of Korea.
2. G3 currency bonds are denominated in either euros, Japanese yen, or United States dollars.
3. Figures were computed based on 31 March 2024 currency exchange rates and do not include currency effects.

Source: *AsianBondsOnline* calculations based on Bloomberg LP data.

---

[7] G3 currency bonds are bonds denominated in either euros, Japanese yen, or United States dollars.

Figure 12: G3 Currency Bond Issuance in Emerging East Asia in the First Quarter of 2024

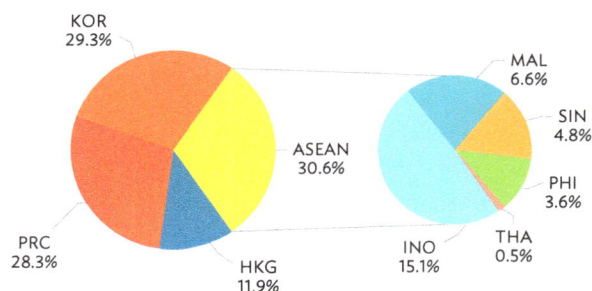

ASEAN = Association of Southeast Asian Nations; HKG = Hong Kong, China; INO = Indonesia; KOR = Republic of Korea; MAL = Malaysia; PHI = Philippines; PRC = People's Republic of China; SIN = Singapore; THA = Thailand.

Notes:
1. Emerging East Asia is defined to include member states of ASEAN plus the People's Republic of China; Hong Kong, China; and the Republic of Korea.
2. G3 currency bonds are denominated in either euros, Japanese yen, or United States dollars.

Source: *AsianBondsOnline* calculations based on Bloomberg LP data.

with USD7.5 billion and USD3.3 billion, respectively. Bank Indonesia was the top issuer of G3 currency bonds in the ASEAN region during Q1 2024, with a USD4.9 billion issuance of zero-coupon, short-term bonds to support the foreign exchange market. Viet Nam did not issue any G3 currency bonds in Q1 2024.

Section 5. Yield Curve Movements

Between 1 March and 31 May, most government bond yields in emerging East Asia rose amid the delay in the expected Federal Reserve rate cut (**Figure 13**). Yield upticks during the review period stemmed from (i) the rise in advanced economy yields as the Federal Reserve delayed its planned rate cut and some Federal Reserve officials issued hawkish statements, (ii) persistent inflation in some regional markets in recent months, and (iii) possible changes in expected domestic monetary policy easing. One exception was the PRC, where bond yields declined, largely driven by a slew of government measures to boost economic growth and support the property sector.

Figure 13: Benchmark Yield Curves—Local Currency Government Bonds

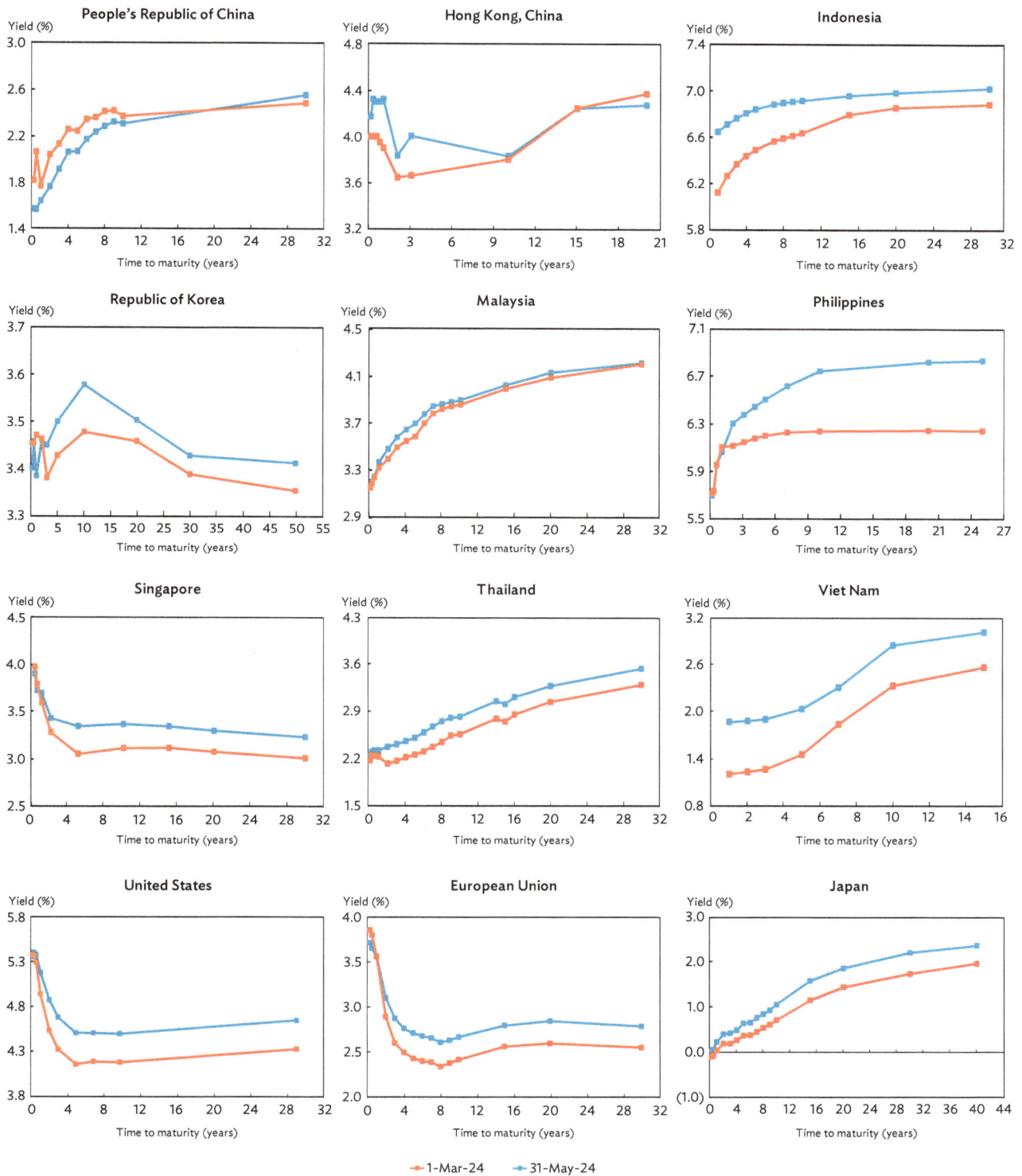

( ) = negative.
Sources: Based on data from Bloomberg LP and Thai Bond Market Association.

Recent Developments in ASEAN+3 Sustainable Bond Markets

The outstanding stock of sustainable bonds in ASEAN+3 economies totaled USD805.9 billion at the end of March.[8] Higher-for-longer interest rates dampened sentiment in the region, leading to less issuance in the first quarter (Q1) of 2024 and resulting in a slowdown in the quarter-on-quarter (q-o-q) growth of bonds outstanding. Hence, the stock of outstanding sustainable bonds in ASEAN+3 economies was only 0.7% greater than at the end of the fourth quarter (Q4) of 2023, but it was 21.4% greater than in March 2023. The year-on-year growth rate for the region's sustainable bond market exceeded growth rates in the European Union 20 (EU-20) (20.4%) and the global market (17.7%). By region, ASEAN+3 remained the second-largest sustainable bond market in the world in Q1 2024, with a global share of 18.9%, trailing only the EU-20 at 37.6% (**Figure 14**). Despite growth in the

ASEAN+3 market, sustainable bonds accounted for only 2.1% of the region's total bonds outstanding at the end of March. In the EU-20, the corresponding share was 7.3%.

The bulk of ASEAN+3 sustainable bonds are green bonds, denominated in local currency (LCY), and issued by private companies (Figure 15).

- By instrument, green bonds were 64.3% of all sustainable bonds; social bonds, 17.3%; and sustainability bonds, 13.8%.
- By economy, the People's Republic of China (PRC) accounted for 42.8% of the ASEAN+3 sustainable bond market (versus 54.9% of the ASEAN+3 general bond market), while ASEAN economies accounted for 9.1% (versus 6.0%).
- By type of issuer, private sector issuances comprised 72.4% of the market (versus 24.7% in the general market). The public sector, despite sustainable bonds'

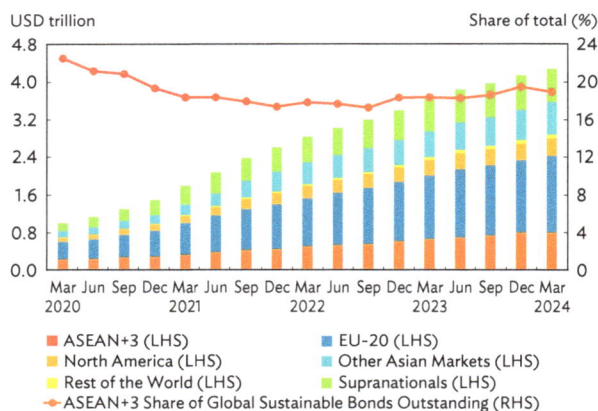

Figure 14: Global Sustainable Bonds Outstanding

ASEAN+3 = Association of Southeast Asian Nations plus the People's Republic of China; Hong Kong, China; Japan; and the Republic of Korea; EU-20 = European Union 20; LHS = left-hand side; RHS = right-hand side; USD = United States dollar.

Notes:
1. EU-20 includes European Union member markets Austria, Belgium, Croatia, Cyprus, Estonia, Finland, France, Germany, Greece, Ireland, Italy, Latvia, Lithuania, Luxembourg, Malta, the Netherlands, Portugal, Slovakia, Slovenia, and Spain.
2. Data include both local currency and foreign currency issues.

Source: *AsianBondsOnline* calculations based on Bloomberg LP data.

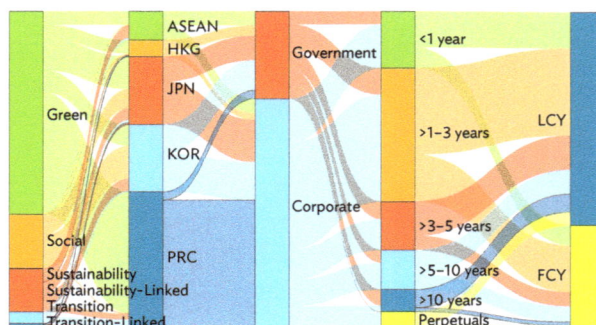

Figure 15: Market Profile of Outstanding ASEAN+3 Sustainable Bonds at the End of March 2024

ASEAN = Association of Southeast Asian Nations; FCY = foreign currency; HKG = Hong Kong, China; JPN = Japan; KOR = Republic of Korea; LCY = local currency; PRC = People's Republic of China.

Notes:
1. ASEAN+3 is defined to include member states of ASEAN plus the People's Republic of China; Hong Kong, China; Japan; and the Republic of Korea.
2. ASEAN comprises the markets of Cambodia, Indonesia, the Lao People's Democratic Republic, Malaysia, the Philippines, Singapore, Thailand, and Viet Nam.

Source: *AsianBondsOnline* calculations based on Bloomberg LP data.

---

[8] ASEAN+3 is defined to include member states of the Association of Southeast Asian Nations (ASEAN) plus the People's Republic of China; Hong Kong, China; Japan; and the Republic of Korea.

potential in aiding governments' development goals, is not a significant issuer.

- By currency, LCY-denominated bonds were 67.5% of the market (versus 95.5% in the general market).[9]

Short-term tenors dominate the ASEAN+3 sustainable bond market, but there are notable differences between ASEAN and non-ASEAN economies in average tenors. At the end of Q1 2024, 75.6% of ASEAN+3 sustainable bonds had maturities of less than 5 years (compared to 46.2% in the EU-20) (**Figure 16**). The size-weighted average tenor of sustainable bonds in ASEAN+3 was 4.2 years, compared to 7.5 years in the ASEAN+3 general bond market and 8.0 years in the EU-20 sustainable bond market. There also is heterogeneity across ASEAN+3 markets. Sustainable bonds with maturities longer than 5 years comprised 65.2% of the total in ASEAN markets but only 20.3% in the four non-ASEAN economies (**Figure 17**). Consequently, the size-weighted average tenor in ASEAN was 10.9 years, compared with only 3.5 years in the non-ASEAN economies. The dominance of long tenors in ASEAN markets is attributed to the active participation by and rising awareness of the public sector in sustainable bond issuance, which is due to larger public deficits and higher investment requirements versus non-ASEAN

Figure 17: Maturity Profiles of ASEAN+3 and European Union 20 Sustainable Bonds Outstanding at the End of March 2024

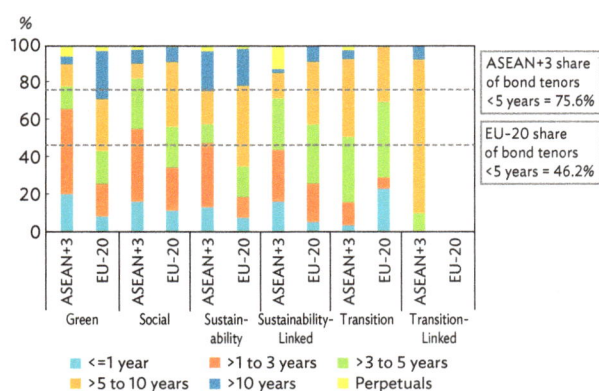

ASEAN+3 = Association of Southeast Asian Nations plus the People's Republic of China; Hong Kong, China; Japan; and the Republic of Korea; EU-20 = European Union 20; HKG = Hong Kong, China; JPN = Japan; KOR = Republic of Korea; PRC = People's Republic of China.
Notes:
1. The EU-20 includes European Union member markets Austria, Belgium, Croatia, Cyprus, Estonia, Finland, France, Germany, Greece, Ireland, Italy, Latvia, Lithuania, Luxembourg, Malta, the Netherlands, Portugal, Slovakia, Slovenia, and Spain.
2. Data include both local currency and foreign currency issues.
Source: *AsianBondsOnline* computations based on Bloomberg LP data.

economies. In particular, Indonesia and Thailand have regularly issued sustainable bonds through Treasury auctions, while Singapore has included green bond issuance as part of its Singapore Green Plan 2030. In contrast, in the larger and more developed non-ASEAN bond markets, it is much easier for corporates to access debt financing.

Sustainable bond issuance in ASEAN+3 declined on a q-o-q basis in Q1 2024 on expectations of higher-for-longer interest rates in the US and the region. Issuance in ASEAN+3 totaled USD49.7 billion, or 13.3% less than in Q4 2023. In contrast, global sustainable bond issuance of USD276.0 billion was up 54.6% q-o-q, mainly due to large issuances in the EU-20 as the European Central Bank has been relatively dovish compared with the Federal Reserve. The EU-20 also continues to promote sustainable bond financing. For example, on 24 October 2023, the Council of the European Union established regulations for the creation of an EU green bond standard, and on 1 January 2024, the first part of the European Sustainability Reporting Standards took effect. As a result, ASEAN+3 sustainable bond issuance shrank from 32.1% of the global total in Q4 2023 to 18.0% in Q1 2024 (**Figure 18**). By instrument, issuance of green bonds and social bonds in Q1 2024 declined the most compared

Figure 16: Maturity Profiles of ASEAN+3 and European Union 20 Sustainable Bonds Outstanding by Type of Bond at the End of March 2024

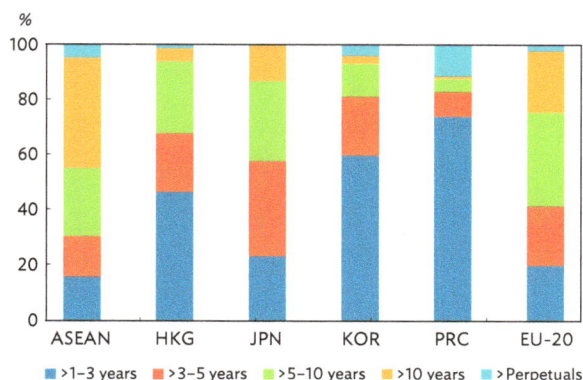

ASEAN+3 = Association of Southeast Asian Nations plus the People's Republic of China; Hong Kong, China; Japan; and the Republic of Korea; EU-20 = European Union 20.
Notes:
1. EU-20 includes European Union member markets Austria, Belgium, Croatia, Cyprus, Estonia, Finland, France, Germany, Greece, Ireland, Italy, Latvia, Lithuania, Luxembourg, Malta, the Netherlands, Portugal, Slovakia, Slovenia, and Spain.
2. Data include both local currency and foreign currency issues.
Source: *AsianBondsOnline* calculations based on Bloomberg LP data.

[9] In the EU-20, in contrast, the shares of LCY bonds were about the same in the sustainable bond market (89.9%) and the general market (90.5%).

Figure 18: ASEAN+3 Sustainable Bond Issuance and Share of Global Sustainable Bond Issuance

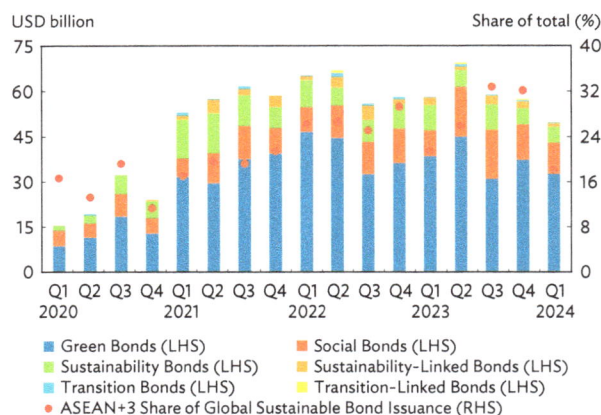

ASEAN+3 = Association of Southeast Asian Nations plus the People's Republic of China; Hong Kong, China; Japan; and the Republic of Korea; LHS = left-hand side; Q1 = first quarter; Q2 = second quarter; Q3 = third quarter; Q4 = fourth quarter; RHS = right-hand side; USD = United States dollar.
Note: Data include both local currency and foreign currency issues.
Source: *AsianBondsOnline* calculations based on Bloomberg LP data.

Figure 19: Market Profile of ASEAN+3 Sustainable Bond Issuance in the First Quarter of 2024

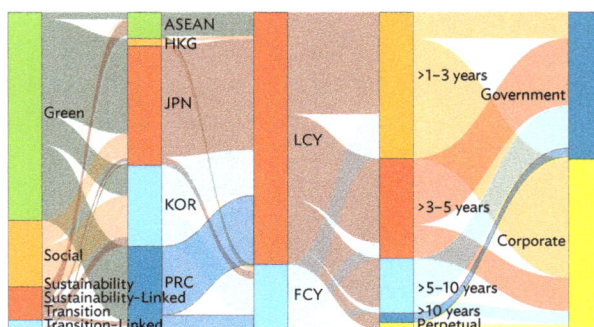

ASEAN = Association of Southeast Asian Nations; FCY = foreign currency; HKG = Hong Kong, China; JPN = Japan; KOR = Republic of Korea; LCY = local currency; PRC = People's Republic of China.
Notes:
1. ASEAN+3 is defined to include member states of ASEAN plus the People's Republic of China; Hong Kong, China; Japan; and the Republic of Korea.
2. ASEAN comprises the markets of Indonesia, Malaysia, the Philippines, Singapore, Thailand, and Viet Nam.
Source: *AsianBondsOnline* calculations based on Bloomberg LP data.

to Q4 2023. By economy of origin, Japan accounted for 37.5% of total issuance in ASEAN+3, followed by the PRC (26.4%) and the Republic of Korea (25.6%). The bulk of issuances in the markets of Japan and the PRC were in green bonds, while for the Republic of Korea, it was social bonds. Only Japan and the Republic of Korea posted q-o-q increases in issuance in Q1 2024.

LCY instruments and short-term financing dominated issuance in ASEAN+3 in Q1 2024 (Figure 19).

- By currency, LCY-denominated bonds comprised 79.3% of the regional issuance total, although this was less than their 96.4% share in the general bond market.[10]
- By maturity, issuances maturing in 5 years or less comprised 77.4% of the issuance total in ASEAN+3, compared with 34.2% in the EU-20. The size-weighted average tenor of issuances was 5.0 years, compared with 9.7 years in the EU-20 and 6.4 years in the ASEAN+3 general bond market. Regarding the share of issuances with tenors longer than 5 years, Japan had the highest share (42.6%) in ASEAN+3, followed by ASEAN members (37.9%).
- By issuer, corporates accounted for 53.9% of total issuance, with the public sector responsible for the remaining 46.1%. Firms from the financial sector

Figure 20: ASEAN+3 Sustainable Bond Issuance by Industry Sector in the First Quarter of 2024

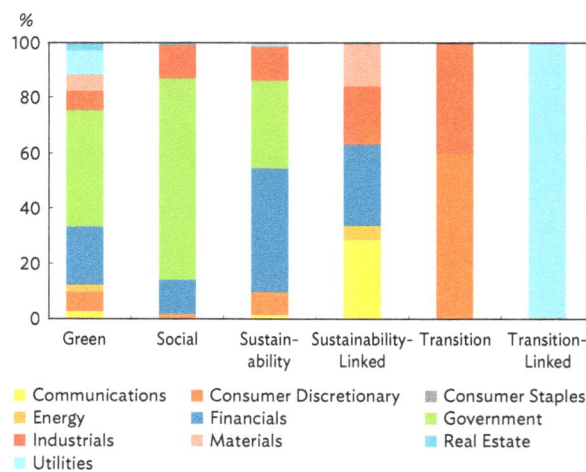

Notes:
1. ASEAN+3 is defined to include member states of the Association of Southeast Asian Nations plus the People's Republic of China; Hong Kong, China; Japan; and the Republic of Korea.
2. Data include both local currency and foreign currency issues.
Source: *AsianBondsOnline* computations based on Bloomberg LP data.

were the largest private sustainable bond issuers, accounting for 21.9% of the regional issuance total (**Figure 20**).

---

[10] In the EU-20, LCY-denominated bonds account for about 86% of issuances in both the sustainable and general bond markets.

Policy and Regulatory Developments

People's Republic of China

State Council Releases Guidelines on Capital Market Development

On 12 April, the State Council released guidelines to facilitate development of the capital market. The guidelines are focused on strengthening capital market regulation, reducing risk, and deepening the capital market. The guidelines aim for a well-regulated, transparent, and resilient capital market through increased regulation of securities issuance and listing, enhanced oversight of underwriting firms, and monitoring of listed companies.

Hong Kong, China

Hong Kong, China's Government Expands Green Bond Program to Include Sustainable Bonds; Sets up Infrastructure Bond Program

Effective 10 May, Hong Kong, China's Government Green Bond Programme was renamed the Government Sustainable Bond Programme in view of the program's expansion to cover sustainable bonds. Furthermore, an Infrastructure Bond Program was established for major infrastructure projects. Both actions were proposed by the government's financial secretary in February as part of the financial year 2024–2025 budget. The Legislative Council passed a resolution on 8 May that authorized the government to borrow up to HKD500 billion under the Infrastructure Bond Programme and the Government Sustainable Bond Programme, thus providing the legal basis for both programs. The two programs will gradually replace the existing Government Bond Program, with details to be announced in due course.

Hong Kong Monetary Authority Extends Green and Sustainable Finance Grant through 2027

On 3 May, the Hong Kong Monetary Authority released details of the extended Green and Sustainable Finance Grant Scheme and published the updated guidelines for grant applications. The grant, originally set to operate from May 2021 to May 2024, provided support for eligible green and sustainable bonds issued in Hong Kong, China. Following the financial secretary's proposal in the financial year 2024–2025 budget, the scheme was extended for 3 years through financial year 2026–2027. As with the original grant, the extended scheme provides a subsidy for general bond issuance costs and external review costs. The extended scheme expands the grant scope to include transition bonds and loans as eligible financial instruments.

Indonesia

Government Conducts Debt Switch

In March, the Government of Indonesia conducted a bond switch amounting to IDR2,474 billion. The eligible bonds for the debt switch had varying maturities ranging from 3 months to 4 years, while the destination bonds carried maturities ranging from 10 years to 20 years. With the bond switch, the government was able to extend the debt repayment schedule for eligible maturing bonds. The government will have another debt switch transaction scheduled on 26 September of this year.

Government of Indonesia to Issue IDR170 Trillion of Treasury Bonds in the Second Quarter of 2024

In April, the Government of Indonesia announced plans to raise IDR170.0 trillion via the auction of Treasury bonds in the second quarter of 2024, which is less than the target issuance of IDR230.9 trillion in the first quarter. The issuance during the second quarter will comprise both conventional and Islamic bonds, with auctions scheduled in alternating weeks. The bonds to be issued will carry maturities ranging from 3 months to 30 years. The government noted that the schedule, bond offering, and auction amount may be subject to adjustments depending on market conditions, investor demand, and financing strategy.

Republic of Korea

The Republic of Korea Remains on the Watch List for Inclusion in the FTSE World Government Bond Index

In March, the Government of the Republic of Korea announced that it was still on the watch list for inclusion in the FTSE World Government Bond Index. It also highlighted that FTSE Russell acknowledged the notable progress and efforts made by the government to improve foreign investors' accessibility to the government bond market. Among the reforms made were the implementation of tax exemption on the income derived from foreign investors' investments in government bonds starting January 2023 and the abolishment of the Investor Registration Certificate starting December 2023. The government will implement more reforms in line with attaining inclusion in the index this year such as (i) the opening of omnibus accounts for government bonds linked with the International Central Securities Depositories in June 2024 to encourage foreign investors to invest via Euroclear or Eurostream, and (ii) other programs to improve foreign exchange transactions related to investments and the trading of government bonds.

Malaysia

Bank Negara Malaysia Strengthens the Ringgit

On 8 April, Bank Negara Malaysia's Financial Markets Committee released a statement updating investors on positive developments in the central bank's efforts to support the Malaysian ringgit. In February, the Malaysian ringgit recorded its lowest level against the United States (US) dollar since the 1997–1998 Asian financial crisis. In its statement, the committee noted the ringgit's appreciation against the US dollar between 26 February and 8 April, as well as the high average daily foreign exchange volume during this period due to organized efforts by the central bank and government-linked institutions. Bank Negara Malaysia assessed that these efforts were sustainable and capable of encouraging foreign-exchange-related activities by corporations in Malaysia.

Philippines

Financial Stability Coordination Council to Strengthen the Corporate Bond Market in 2024

During its 38th executive committee meeting held early this year, Financial Stability Coordination Council (FSCC) Chairman and Bangko Sentral ng Pilipinas Governor Eli M. Remolona, Jr. acknowledged the strength of the Philippines' financial markets despite global geopolitical risks. He noted that current market behavior aligns with a "risk-on" stance, indicating market optimism and low perceived risks, which is expected to foster economic activity. The FSCC anticipates an increase in corporations' funding requirements during the "risk-on" phase as a significant amount of corporate bonds and loans are set to mature in 2024, prompting the need for refinancing. While the banking system can accommodate increased funding demand, the FSCC emphasized the importance of a viable and competitive corporate bond market. The FSCC plans to engage different market constituents to deepen the corporate bond market. FSCC's long-term objective is to have a diverse set of corporate bond issuers and active risk-pricing for outstanding bonds. An active corporate bond market benefits all credit categories of borrowers as it widens funding access, provides opportunities for investors with varying risk appetites, and enhances overall risk management.

Singapore

Singapore and Japan Renew Bilateral Swap Agreement

On 21 May, the Monetary Authority of Singapore and the Bank of Japan renewed their bilateral swap agreement. Under this arrangement, Singapore can swap Singapore dollars for the equivalent of up to USD3 billion of Japanese yen or US dollars, while Japan can exchange Japanese yen with Singapore for up to USD1 billion. The agreement aims to strengthen the relationship and financial stability of both markets.

Thailand

Government Conducts THB80 Billion Bond Switch

In May, the Government of Thailand conducted bond switch transactions involving THB80.0 billion worth of government bonds. The transactions allowed investors to exchange eligible source bonds that were maturing soon with selected destination bonds that had longer remaining maturities. The five source bonds had remaining maturities ranging from 0.3 year to 2.1 years, while the seven destination bonds had remaining tenors from 4.8 years to 48.1 years. The bond switch allowed the government to reduce its short-term debt obligations, extending the average maturity of outstanding debt, and created liquidity in the market. Investor groups that participated in the transactions included the Government Pension Fund, commercial banks, insurance companies, various government and private funds, and some foreign investors.

Viet Nam

Government Plans to Borrow VND120 Trillion in the Second Quarter 2024

The Government of Viet Nam plans to raise VND120.0 trillion in the second quarter of 2024 through its Treasury bonds offering. The planned issuance was 5.5% lower than the VND127.0 trillion borrowing plan in the previous quarter. Treasury bonds to be auctioned will carry tenors of 5–30 years and auctions are scheduled every Wednesday. Of the VND120.0 trillion borrowing planned for the second quarter of 2024, the government had already raised a total of VND45.8 trillion as of 22 May, comprising 38.1% of the quarterly borrowing target.

Environmental Materiality in eXtensible Business Reporting Language Disclosures: Evidence from Japan

Surging environmental, social, and governance (ESG) investment drives have increased demand for more information on companies' sustainability performance.[11] As a useful instrument for investors to obtain information, ESG ratings are crucial for measuring a company's adherence to sustainability principles. However, the cost of purchasing ESG ratings has made them difficult for the public to access. Furthermore, mixed evidence—including the latest study conducted by Managi, Xie, and Yoshida (2024)—has shown that ESG ratings are not consistent across different rating agencies.[12]

An alternative approach to gathering companies' sustainability-related information is through companies' self-disclosure. In Japan, large, listed companies often report their ESG data through integrated reports or sustainability reports. Meanwhile, annual securities reports—the disclosure of which is compulsory for all listed companies in Japan—also convey companies' ESG information. These reports are published using eXtensible Business Reporting Language (XBRL), a computer language format used in business reporting. The machine-readable nature of XBRL allows for the standardized electronic sharing of business, financial, and nonfinancial information, and improves the accessibility and comparability of the information. The standardized format of XBRL disclosure ensures that ESG information from annual securities reports offers greater transparency and comparability than other company documents, making its use more efficient and effective for investors, regulators, and other stakeholders.

By analyzing the text data from XBRL-disclosed annual securities reports of around 3,800 listed companies in

Japan from 2013 to 2023, this study aims to uncover the trend of Japanese corporate ESG materiality disclosure, particularly the environmental aspects. Furthermore, this research explores the potential of self-disclosed ESG information based on XBRL technology as an alternative source for predicting companies' sustainability and financial performance.

The use of ESG-related keywords in the annual securities reports of Japanese publicly listed firms increased from 2013 to 2023. **Table 3** shows that Japanese corporates' self-disclosure of ESG activities has evolved over the years. A transition from phrases like "raw materials" to "recycling," "climate change," and "renewable energy" illustrates a strategic move toward sustainable production, energy solutions, and addressing global warming. At the materiality level, a notable increase in environmental materiality disclosures was observed during the review period (**Figure 21**). This progression highlights a pivotal shift in corporate priorities toward embracing comprehensive sustainability strategies and ethical business practices in response to global environmental challenges.

Meanwhile, ESG materiality disclosures are not isolated incidents but rather are interlinked, revealing a corporate shift toward addressing ESG issues in a holistic manner. The correlation analysis of the frequency of occurrence of corporates' self-disclosure of ESG materialities reveals a nuanced interplay between environmental initiatives and social and governance initiatives. Specifically, there are increasing trends of correlation between disclosure of (i) environmental materiality and social materiality (**Figure 22a**), (ii) environmental materiality

---

[11] This note was written by Jiaqi Yang and Kotaro Takahashi from Sustainable Lab Inc., and by Satoru Yamadera and Shu Tian from the Asian Development Bank. This note is a nontechnical summary of a forthcoming working paper titled "ESG Materiality in XBRL (eXtensible Business Reporting Language) Disclosures and its Performance Predictability: Evidence from Japan" that was written by a joint research team from Sustainable Lab Inc. and the Asian Development Bank.

[12] Managi, Shunsuke, Jun Xie, and Kenichi Yoshida. 2024. "Environmental, Social, and Governance Performance and Its Financial Impacts: A Comparative Analysis of Companies in Asia." *Asia Bond Monitor March 2024*.

Table 3: Environment-Related Keywords in the Annual Securities Reports of Japanese Listed Firms by Frequency of Occurrence, 2013–2023

Environment-related keywords have increasingly appeared in the annual securities reports of listed Japanese companies since 2013.

Financial Year	Top 1		Top 2		Top 3		Top 4		Top 5	
	Keyword	FO	Keyword	FO	Keyword	FO	Keyword	FO	Keyword	FO
2013	Raw Materials	269	Natural Disasters	267	Production Base	46	Recycling	30	Water Quality	28
2014	Natural Disasters	3,121	Raw Materials	3,009	Production Base	662	Recycling	512	Energy Conservation	328
2015	Natural Disasters	3,326	Raw Materials	3,120	Production Base	672	Recycling	510	Energy Conservation	319
2016	Natural Disasters	3,655	Raw Materials	3,198	Production Base	676	Recycling	514	Energy Conservation	304
2017	Natural Disasters	3,971	Raw Materials	3,588	Production Base	959	Recycling	685	Renewable Energy	473
2018	Natural Disasters	4,504	Raw Materials	3,939	Production Base	1,000	Recycling	820	Renewable Energy	572
2019	Natural Disasters	4,953	Raw Materials	4,083	Production Base	1,016	Recycling	905	Renewable Energy	649
2020	Natural Disasters	7,324	Raw Materials	6,209	Supply Chain	1,928	Production Base	1,516	Recycling	1,333
2021	Natural Disasters	7,220	Raw Materials	6,868	Climate Change	2,479	Supply Chain	2,404	Renewable Energy	1,667
2022	Raw Materials	11,447	Natural Disasters	7,742	Climate Change	6,006	Supply Chain	4,218	Carbon Neutral	2,256
2023	Climate Change	15,515	Raw Materials	10,888	Natural Disasters	6,811	Supply Chain	4,706	Carbon Neutral	3,986

FO = frequency of occurrence.

Source: Authors' calculations based on annual securities reports from over 3,800 listed companies in Japan released in eXtensible Business Reporting Language format.

Figure 21: Share of Listed Companies in Japan Disclosing Environmental Materiality, 2013–2023

Environmental materiality disclosure of listed Japanese companies has steadily increased since 2014.

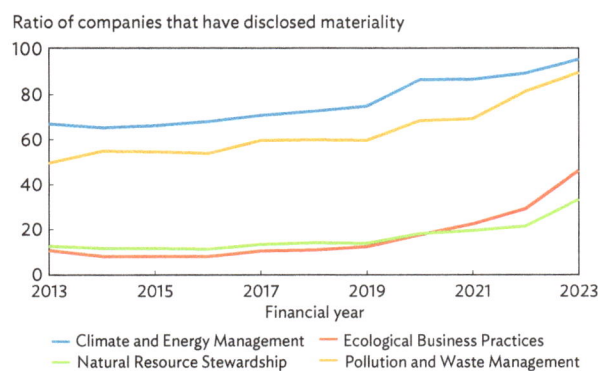

Source: Authors' calculations based on annual securities reports from over 3,800 listed companies in Japan released in eXtensible Business Reporting Language format.

and governance materiality (**Figure 22b**), and (iii) social materiality and governance materiality (**Figure 22c**). Taken tighter, these findings indicate a proactive shift in corporate strategies toward blending environmental, social, and governance concerns into a unified operational framework.

There is, however, limited evidence to show that ESG materiality in corporate disclosure contains useful information related to corporates' financial or climate performances. A fixed-effects panel regression was conducted to investigate the relationship between four environmental materiality disclosure measures and several proxies measuring corporate financial performance. The results merely show that companies disclosing climate change and energy management are more likely to be financially robust, as evidenced by their significant association with Altman's Z-score,

---

Figure 22: Correlations among Environmental, Social, and Governance Materiality Disclosure, 2014–2023

The correlations of materiality disclosure between E and S, E and G, and S and G have increased for listed Japanese companies since 2014, implying ESG materiality disclosure is becoming more interlinked.

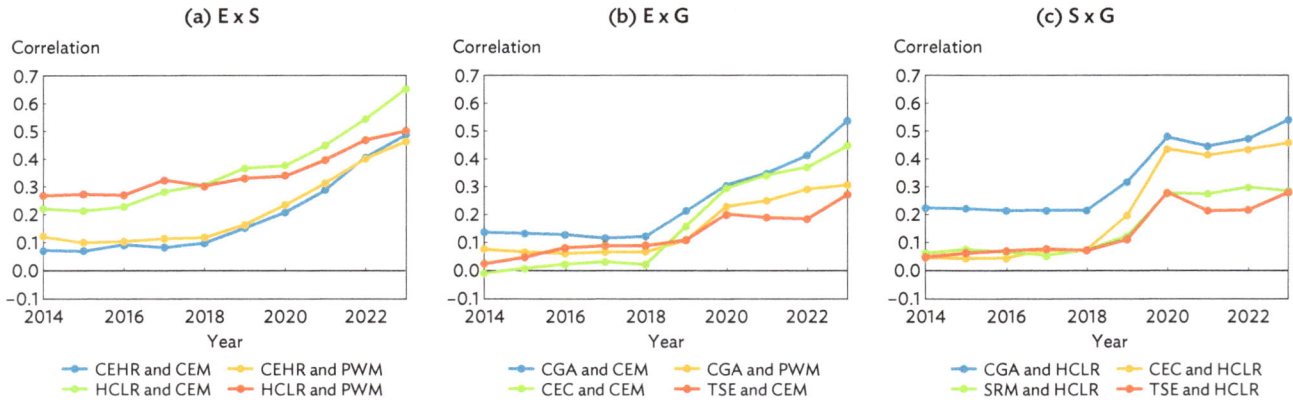

(a) E x S

(b) E x G

(c) S x G

CEHR and CEM   CEHR and PWM
HCLR and CEM   HCLR and PWM

CGA and CEM   CGA and PWM
CEC and CEM   TSE and CEM

CGA and HCLR   CEC and HCLR
SRM and HCLR   TSE and HCLR

CEC = corporate ethics and compliance; CEHR = community engagement and human rights; CEM = climate and energy management; CGA= corporate governance and accountability; E = environmental; ESG = environmental, social, and governance; G = governance; HCLR = human capital and labor rights; PWM = pollution and waste management; S = social; SRM = strategic risk management; TSE= transparency and stakeholder engagement.
Source: Authors' calculations based on annual securities reports from over 3,800 listed companies in Japan released in eXtensible Business Reporting Language format.

---

a proxy measuring a company's risk level (**Figure 23**). Moreover, most of the 12 ESG materiality disclosure measurements are not significantly related to corporate climate performance. One exception is that companies' engagement in strategic risk management is negatively and significantly related to emissions intensity, which is measured by total greenhouse gas emissions per sale (**Figure 24a**) and per asset (**Figure 24b**).

This study finds that companies' self-disclosure of ESG materiality alone is insufficient as a standalone measure to evaluate and predict financial profitability and climate performance, despite the increasing trend of disclosure being observed from the text data released in XBRL format. This study offers evidence-based insights for corporations, investors, and regulatory bodies in regional markets on the importance of understanding the informativeness of current ESG disclosure practices, as well as the necessity to explore comparable and cost-efficient ways besides self-disclosed ESG data to gather corporate performance-related information and enhance transparency in ESG finance markets.

Figure 23: Fixed-Effects Panel Regression Results—Impact of Environmental Materiality Disclosure on Corporate Financial Performance

The potential of corporate self-disclosure of environmental materiality to predict corporate financial performance is limited, as only the category of climate and energy management is significantly related to Altman's Z-score.

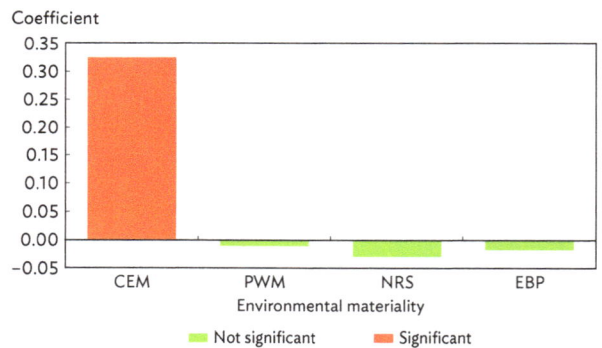

CEM = climate and energy management, EBP = ecological business practices, NRS = natural resource stewardship, PWM = pollution and waste management.
Note: Altman's Z-score is used as a proxy for corporate financial performance.
Source: Authors' calculations based on annual securities reports from over 3,800 listed companies in Japan released in eXtensible Business Reporting Language format.

Figure 24: Fixed-Effects Panel Regression Results—Impact of Environmental, Social, and Governance Materiality Disclosure on Corporate Financial Performance

The potential of corporate self-disclosure of ESG materiality to predict corporate climate performance is limited, as most of the relationships are not statistically significant.

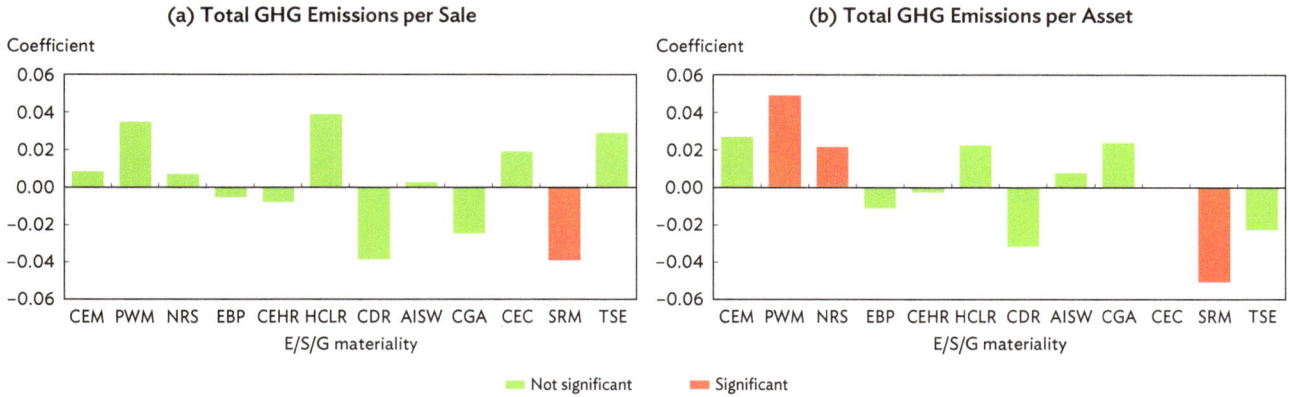

(a) Total GHG Emissions per Sale

(b) Total GHG Emissions per Asset

AISW = access inclusivity and social welfare; CDR = customer and digital responsibility; CEC = corporate ethics and compliance; CEHR = community engagement and human rights; CEM = climate and energy management; CGA= corporate governance and accountability; E = environmental; EBP = ecological business practices; ESG = environmental, social, and governance; G = governance; GHG = greenhouse gas; HCLR = human capital and labor rights; NRS = natural resource stewardship; PWM = pollution and waste management; S = social; SRM = strategic risk management; TSE= transparency and stakeholder engagement.

Note: Coefficient is significant if p-value is less than 0.05.

Source: Authors' calculations based on annual securities reports from over 3,800 listed companies in Japan released in eXtensible Business Reporting Language format.

Taxonomies in Action: The ASEAN Taxonomy for Sustainable Finance

The Rise of Taxonomies

In orienting capital toward sustainability and sustainable economic activities, including climate action, the important question of where financing should be directed and what would qualify for financing and investment to meet the sustainability agenda has arisen.[13] Taxonomies, which can be described in simple terms as comprehensive classification systems, can provide a common language in identifying sustainable activities. This common language works in the same way we order coffee around the world. Because there is a common language around coffee, a cappuccino has steamed milk and foam, and not whipped cream, whether it is in Thailand or in Ecuador. The common language from a taxonomy is critical in

- providing a consistent language and reference for different stakeholders;
- helping businesses and project owners understand what they need to do to be eligible for sustainable financing;
- supporting risk management and strategic decision-making; and
- converting undertakings and pledges, such as the Paris Agreement or national pledges, into tangible action including through guiding government policy and market action.

A taxonomy's approach and assessment criteria need to be contextualized to address national circumstances, including different starting points, economic and social circumstances, and resources. This has resulted in the proliferation of taxonomies, which necessitates embedding interoperability into their design. There are currently more than 50 official taxonomies (national and regional) that have been developed or are in development, not including private sector guidance. The European Union (EU) Taxonomy for sustainable activities is an official taxonomy that applies to the EU, the Association of Southeast Asian Nations Taxonomy for Sustainable Finance (ASEAN Taxonomy) represents a common language for a region, and the Climate Bonds Initiative Taxonomy is an example of a proprietary or market taxonomy. Japan does not have a taxonomy but instead uses sector roadmaps that provide direction for a transition toward achieving carbon neutrality by 2050 for greenhouse-gas-intensive industries. The Korean Green Taxonomy was issued in 2021 as a voluntary taxonomy, while the China Green Bond Endorsed Projects Catalogue, also issued in 2021, is mandatory.

Sustainable finance taxonomies can cover different elements of sustainability including sustainable activities (sustainability), the environment (green), and social aspects (social). As such, while a taxonomy can be classified based on its predominant element, it should not be "boxed in" as only containing that element.

Some taxonomies are based on the performance outcomes of economic activities (e.g., ASEAN, the EU, the Republic of Korea, the Philippines), while others prescribe what is eligible for investments (e.g., Bangladesh, the People's Republic of China, Kazakhstan, and Mongolia). The former are referred to as technical screening criteria (TSC)-based or principles-based taxonomies, while the latter are known as whitelist taxonomies. The "traffic light" approach is a common example of a multi-classification approach using the common categories of green (meets ambition or criteria), amber (transitioning), and red (ineligible). Multiple classifications are helpful in providing an avenue to incorporate transition into taxonomies.

Taxonomies and Transition

It is unrealistic to decarbonize immediately as there are hard-to-abate sectors, economic activities with no technologically or economically feasible low-carbon alternatives, infrastructure bottlenecks, and the risk of

---

[13] This write-up was prepared by Eugene Wong (chief executive officer) of Sustainable Finance Institute Asia.

economic and social dislocations for economies that are not sufficiently resourced or ready. As such, transition is necessary. Transitions are increasingly being recognized as key to driving the sustainability agenda, and there is a need to consider how to incorporate transition into taxonomies. Incorporating transitions often results in a "traffic light" system where a specific amber classification is applied.

All taxonomies in the ASEAN region incorporate specific transition categories, making them transition taxonomies. The ASEAN Taxonomy for example, explicitly recognizes transition by

- using a multi-tiered approach for its TSC that includes a green tier reflecting the taxonomy's climate ambition that is, wherever possible, benchmarked to the EU Taxonomy, together with two tiers carrying amber classifications that provide a progressive pathway to transition toward green; and
- including the concept of "remedial measures to transition" to provide real economy participants with the opportunity to progress on a pathway to green while being allowed a specified timeframe to incorporate remediation measures to mitigate the harm caused to an environmental objective in the pursuit of another.

When incorporating transition into taxonomies, it is important to ensure that safeguards are incorporated to avoid investments being directed toward the development or improvement of high-emitting assets, or scenarios where the desired investments are made only at the tail end of the transition period.

The Association of Southeast Asian Nations Taxonomy

The ASEAN Finance Ministers and Central Bank Governors' Meeting endorsed the establishment of the ASEAN Taxonomy Board to develop, maintain, and promote a multi-tiered taxonomy that considers ASEAN's needs, as well as international aspirations and goals. The ASEAN Taxonomy is to serve as the overarching guide for all ASEAN Member States (AMS), complementing their respective national sustainability initiatives and serving as ASEAN's common language for sustainable finance. The ASEAN Taxonomy was envisaged from the outset to be multi-tiered for inclusivity and to be beneficial to all AMS. It is also intended to facilitate an orderly and effective transition toward a sustainable ASEAN.

The ASEAN Taxonomy is multi-tiered in two ways, which is a hallmark of the taxonomy. The first is that the ASEAN Taxonomy has a principles-based framework known as the Foundation Framework, as well as a TSC-based frame called the Plus Standard. This optionality ensures that every AMS can start classifying economic activities and projects based on their own state of readiness using either of the frames. The second is that each economic activity under the Plus Standard can have up to three performance thresholds, allowing users to start with a tier that is practical for them. This is different from taxonomies that only have one threshold, resulting in an activity being either aligned or not aligned with the relevant taxonomy. Emerging and developing economies can consider using a principles-based taxonomy as a first step toward the eventual adoption of a TSC-based taxonomy as well as the use of multiple tiers for TSCs.

The ASEAN Taxonomy Board identified six economic sectors that contribute to 85% of the greenhouse gas emissions in the ASEAN region. These six sectors, together with three enabling sectors that support the achievement of the ASEAN Taxonomy's four environmental objectives, are covered by the Plus Standard. The ASEAN Taxonomy is currently in its third iteration. The structure of the ASEAN Taxonomy Version 3 is summarized in **Figure 25**.

The ASEAN Taxonomy has four environmental objectives and three essential criteria. To be aligned to the ASEAN Taxonomy, an economic activity should contribute primarily to an environmental objective and meet all three essential criteria. An economic activity can be assessed using either the principles-based Foundation Framework or the TSC-based Plus Standard, depending on which frame has been adopted for that economic activity by the AMS.

The ASEAN Taxonomy Version 3 was issued in March 2024 and currently has TSCs for the electricity, gas, steam, and air conditioning supply (energy); construction and real estate; and transportation and storage focus sectors; as well as a TSC for the carbon capture, utilization, and storage enabling sector. A TSC for coal phase-out was introduced under the energy focus sector, making the ASEAN Taxonomy the first to have a TSC for coal phase-out.

Figure 25: Overview of the Association of Southeast Asian Nations Taxonomy

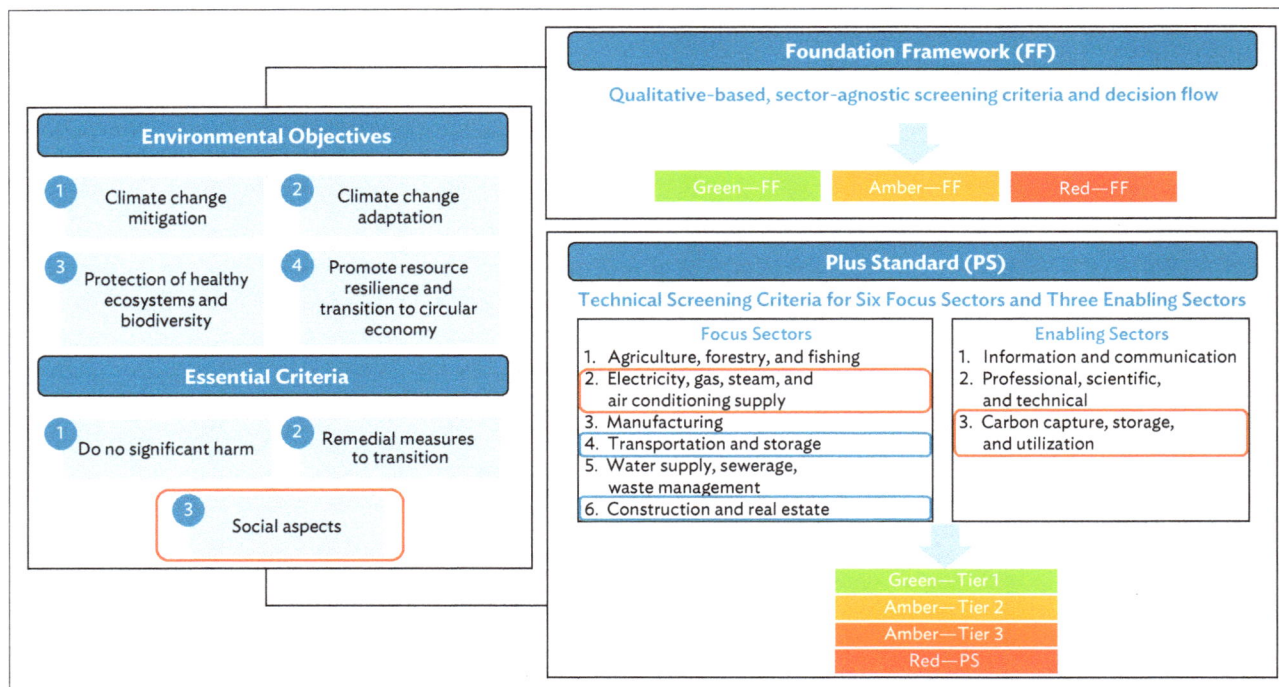

Technical screening criteria (TSC) were added in Version 3.

In Version 2, social aspects were added as an essential criteria and TSC for energy and carbon capture, storage, and utilization released.

Source: Association of Southeast Asian Nations (ASEAN) Taxonomy Board. 2024. *Appendix A: Annex 1 of the ASEAN Taxonomy Version 3*. Jakarta.

The activities under the energy, construction and real estate, and transportation and storage focus sectors are depicted in **Figures 26**, **27**, and **28**, respectively.

The tiered TSC is a distinguishing feature of the ASEAN Taxonomy, and an example of how it is applied is provided in **Table 4**.

Future revisions of the ASEAN Taxonomy will include the remaining three focus sectors and two enabling sectors.

While national taxonomies address national interests and priorities, they should be designed and developed to be as interoperable as possible with globally referenced taxonomies, with variances clearly identified and justified to aid interoperability. The compatibility of the ASEAN Taxonomy and the EU Taxonomy is summarized in **Table 5**.

Several AMS have issued taxonomies, including Bank Negara Malaysia's Climate Change and Principle-based Taxonomy (2021); Securities Commission Malaysia's Principles-Based Sustainable and Responsible Investment Taxonomy (2022); Thailand's Taxonomy Phase 1 (2023); the Singapore–Asia Taxonomy for Sustainable Finance (2023); the Indonesia Taxonomy for Sustainable Finance (2024), which supersedes the Indonesia Green Taxonomy (2022); and the Philippine Sustainable Finance Taxonomy Guidelines (2024). All of these taxonomies are aligned to the ASEAN Taxonomy.

Taxonomies have a very important role to play. Governments and markets must collaborate to ensure that they support, rather than fragment, the sustainability agenda. Eventually, taxonomy equivalence, not just interoperability, will be needed for effective and efficient capital orientation.

Figure 26: Technical Screening Criteria Coverage for Energy Activities

Electricity, gas, steam, and air conditioning supply	13 activities, including • Electricity generation through various means (e.g., solar energy, renewable non-fossil gaseous and liquid fuels, bioenergy, hydropower) • Transmission and distribution (T&D) of electricity • Storage of electricity, including pumped storage • Coal power phase-out
Transmission and distribution networks for renewable and low-carbon gases, including storage of renewable and low-carbon gases	• Transmission and distribution networks for renewable and low-carbon gases • Storage of renewable and low-carbon gases
Production of heating and cooling through various means, including storage of thermal energy	8 activities, including • Production of heating and cooling from various means (e.g., solar thermal energy, renewable non-fossil gaseous and liquid fuels, fossil gas) • Production of heating and cooling using electric heat pump • Production of heating and cooling using waste heat • District heating and cooling distribution • Storage of thermal energy

Source: Author's illustration.

Figure 27: Technical Screening Criteria Coverage for Construction and Real Estate Activities

Buildings	• Acquisition and ownership of buildings • Construction of new buildings • Renovation of existing buildings
Ancillary Activities	• Demolition and site preparation
Technology and Equipment	Installation, maintenance, and repair of • EV charging stations • Energy efficient equipment • Devices for measuring, regulating, and controlling energy performance • Renewable energy technologies • Early warning systems

EV = electric vehicle.
Source: Author's illustration.

Figure 28: Technical Screening Criteria Coverage for Transportation and Storage Activities

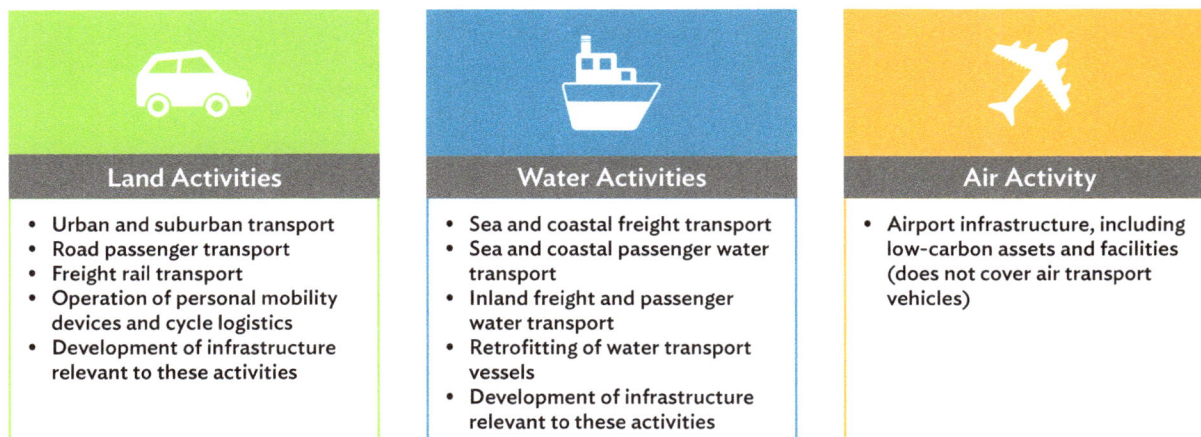

Land Activities

- Urban and suburban transport
- Road passenger transport
- Freight rail transport
- Operation of personal mobility devices and cycle logistics
- Development of infrastructure relevant to these activities

Water Activities

- Sea and coastal freight transport
- Sea and coastal passenger water transport
- Inland freight and passenger water transport
- Retrofitting of water transport vessels
- Development of infrastructure relevant to these activities

Air Activity

- Airport infrastructure, including low-carbon assets and facilities (does not cover air transport vehicles)

Source: Author's illustration.

Table 4: Quantitative Thresholds for the Energy Sector

Tier	EO1: Climate Change Mitigation Threshold	
	ISIC 351: Electricity Generation, Transmission and Distribution, Storage	ISIC 352: Transmission, Distribution and Storage of Renewable and Low-Carbon Gases ISIC 353: Production of Heating/Cooling, Storage of Thermal Energy
Green Tier 1	Lifecycle GHG emissions: <100 gCO_2e/kWh	Lifecycle GHG intensity: <28 gCO_2e/MJ
Amber Tier 2	Lifecycle GHG emissions: ≥100 and <425 gCO_2e/kWh	Lifecycle GHG intensity: <65 gCO_2e/MJ
Amber Tier 3	Lifecycle GHG emissions: ≥425 and <510 gCO_2e/kWh	No TSC available

EO = environmental objective, gCO_2e = grams of carbon dioxide equivalent, ISIC = International Standard Industrial Classification of All Economic Activities, kWh = kilowatt-hour, MJ = megajoule, TSC = technical screening criteria.
Source: Author's compilation.

Table 5: Features and Compatibility of the Association of Southeast Asian Nations and European Union Taxonomies

Feature	ASEAN Taxonomy	EU Taxonomy
Environmental Objective (EO)	1. Climate change mitigation 2. Climate change adaptation 3. Protection of healthy ecosystems and biodiversity 4. Promote resource resilience and transition to circular economy These four EOs encapsulate all six EOs of the EU Taxonomy.	1. Climate change mitigation 2. Climate change adaptation 3. Sustainable use and protection of water and marine resources 4. Transition to a circular economy 5. Pollution prevention and control 6. Protection and restoration of biodiversity and ecosystems
Classification System	ISIC	NACE
Do No Significant Harm (DNSH)	Yes	Yes
Remedial Measures to Transition (RMT)	Yes, to facilitate transition	No
Minimum Safeguards	Yes, social aspects	Yes, alignment with the OECD Guidelines for Multinational Enterprises and the UN Guiding Principles on Business and Human Rights.
Activity classification	Yes, using the Foundation Framework	Straight to TSC
Technical Screening Criteria	Up to three thresholds	Single threshold

ASEAN = Association of Southeast Asian Nations, EU = European Union, ISIC = International Standard Industrial Classification of All Economic Activities, NACE = Statistical Classification of Economic Activities in the European Community, OECD = Organisation for Economic Co-operation and Development, TSC = technical screening criteria, UN = United Nations.
Source: Author's compilation.

Market Summaries

People's Republic of China

Yield Movements

Local currency (LCY) government bond yields in the People's Republic of China (PRC) fell for nearly all maturities between 1 March and 31 May amid continued weakness in the domestic economy as well as low inflation. The PRC's yields experienced a decline, averaging 19 basis points across all maturities that declined. However, the 30-year tenor bucked this trend and saw a 7 basis points increase during the same period, driven by concerns about economic growth despite a higher growth rate of 5.3% year-on-year (y-o-y) in the first quarter (Q1) of 2024 compared to the previous quarter (5.2% y-o-y) (**Figure 1**). Other economic indicators, however, present a different picture. Retail sales fell from 5.1% y-o-y in January–February to 3.1% y-o-y in March, and further to 2.3% y-o-y in April. Weak demand has also dampened inflation, with consumer price inflation hovering near zero at 0.3% y-o-y in April and 0.1% y-o-y in March. Producer price inflation has been in deflation since October 2022. On the other hand, the rise in yields at the long-end of the curve is due to expectations of increased government debt as the government seeks to stimulate the economy. The government announced the planned issuance of CNY1.0 trillion worth of long-term special Treasury bonds as part of its measures to mitigate the impact of weakness in the property market and the economic slowdown. In April, Fitch Ratings revised the PRC's outlook to negative due to economic uncertainties and rising government debt.

Local Currency Bond Market Size and Issuance

The PRC's LCY bonds outstanding grew at a slower quarterly pace in Q1 2024 as government issuance contracted. Total LCY bonds outstanding grew 1.2% quarter-on-quarter (q-o-q) in Q1 2024, down from 1.9% q-o-q in Q4 2023 (**Figure 2**). Growth in government bonds slowed to 1.2% q-o-q in Q1 2024 from 5.7% q-o-q in the previous quarter due to reduced issuance during the period. In contrast, corporate bond growth reached 1.2% q-o-q in Q1 2024, up from −4.9% q-o-q in Q4 2023, on easing measures by the PRC government.

Figure 1: The People's Republic of China's Benchmark Yield Curve—Local Currency Government Bonds

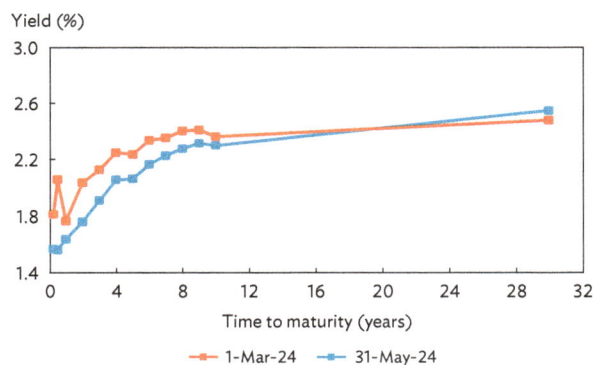

Source: Based on data from Bloomberg LP.

Figure 2: Composition of Local Currency Bonds Outstanding in the People's Republic of China

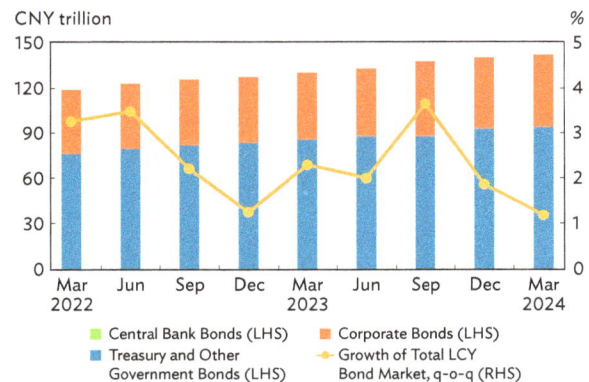

CNY = Chinese yuan, LCY = local currency, LHS = left-hand side, q-o-q = quarter-on-quarter, RHS = right-hand side.
Source: CEIC Data Company.

This market summary was written by Russ Jason Lo, consultant, Economic Research and Development Impact Department, ADB, Manila.

The PRC's LCY bond sales reached CNY9.6 trillion in Q1 2024, a 13.3% q-o-q decline from the previous quarter due to reduced issuance from government entities (**Figure 3**). Overall government issuance declined 24.4% q-o-q in Q1 2024, largely due to a high base effect as efforts by the government to enact stimulus measures led to frontloading of some 2024 issuance quotas in the preceding quarter. Corporate bond issuance, however, rose 3.8% q-o-q in Q1 2024 after a contraction of 12.6% q-o-q in the prior quarter, buoyed by lower borrowing costs following easing measures by the government.

Investor Profile

Commercial banks remained the largest holder of government bonds at the end of March 2024. Commercial banks are the largest investor in the PRC's government bond market, with an overall holdings share of 73.2% at the end of March 2024 (**Figure 4**). Commercial banks are also the dominant holder among all different government bond types, including local government bonds with an 84.8% holdings share.

Sustainable Bond Market

Sustainable bonds in the PRC are mainly green bond instruments, issued by the private sector, and carry shorter-term tenors. The sustainable bond market in the PRC reached a size of USD345.2 billion at the end of March, growing 16.7% from the same period last year. Green bonds comprised 90.4% of total outstanding sustainable bonds at the end of March (**Figure 5**). The majority of sustainable bonds outstanding were issued by private companies, with corporate bonds making up 93.9% of the PRC's sustainable bond market. Corporate issuers tend to issue shorter-tenors compared to the public sector. As a result, 87.1% of the PRC's outstanding sustainable bonds carried tenors of 5 years or less.

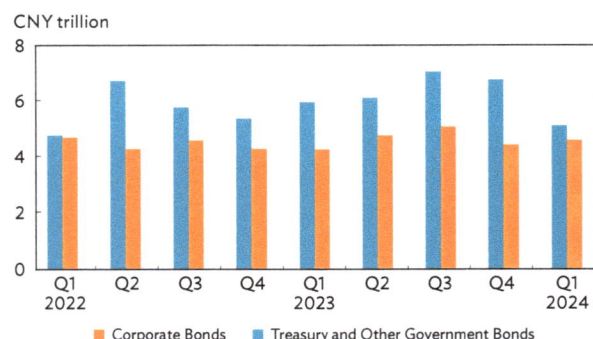

Figure 3: Composition of Local Currency Bond Issuance in the People's Republic of China

CNY = Chinese yuan, Q1 = first quarter, Q2 = second quarter, Q3 = third quarter, Q4 = fourth quarter.
Source: CEIC Data Company.

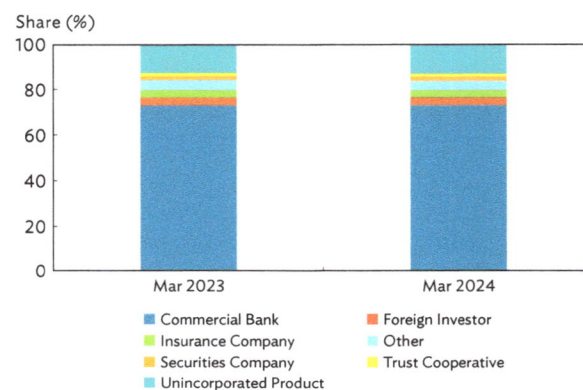

Figure 4: Investor Profile of Government Bonds

Note: Government bonds include bonds issued by local governments, policy banks, and the central government.
Source: CEIC Data Company.

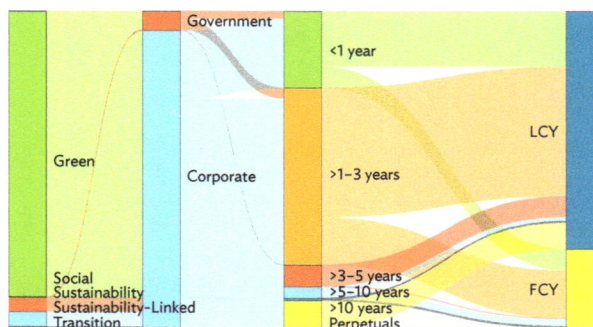

Figure 5: Market Profile of Outstanding Sustainable Bonds in the People's Republic of China at the End of March 2024

FCY = foreign currency, LCY = local currency.
Source: AsianBondsOnline calculations based on Bloomberg LP data.

Hong Kong, China

Yield Movements

Between 1 March and 31 May, local currency (LCY) government bond yields in Hong Kong, China rose for most tenors, driven largely by the delay in the United States Federal Reserve's expected rate cut. Bond yields gained an average of 27 basis points for maturities up to 10 years on market expectations of higher-for-longer interest rates (**Figure 1**). Meanwhile, longer-term bond yields edged down by an average of 5 basis points for tenors of 15–20 years amid a slowdown in domestic economic growth and easing inflation. Hong Kong, China's gross domestic product growth decelerated to 2.7% year-on-year (y-o-y) in the first quarter (Q1) of 2024 from 4.3% y-o-y in the previous quarter. Inflation dropped to 1.1% y-o-y in April from 2.0% y-o-y in March and 2.1% y-o-y in February.

Local Currency Bond Market Size and Issuance

Hong Kong, China's LCY bonds outstanding expanded 0.6% quarter-on-quarter (q-o-q) in Q1 2024, led by growth in corporate bonds. By the end of March, outstanding LCY bonds reached HKD3.0 trillion, driven by a rebound in corporate bonds outstanding, which was supported by large issuances by state-owned entities during the quarter (**Figure 2**). Meanwhile, Hong Kong Special Administrative Region (HKSAR) government bonds recorded modest growth due to small volume of maturities during the quarter. Corporate bonds outstanding (HKD1.5 trillion) comprised 48.9% of Hong Kong, China's LCY bond market at the end of March 2024, while outstanding Exchange Funds Bills and Notes (HKD1.3 trillion) and HKSAR government bonds (HKD0.3 trillion) comprised the remaining 41.7% and 9.4% shares, respectively.

Figure 1: Hong Kong, China's Benchmark Yield Curve—Local Currency Government Bonds

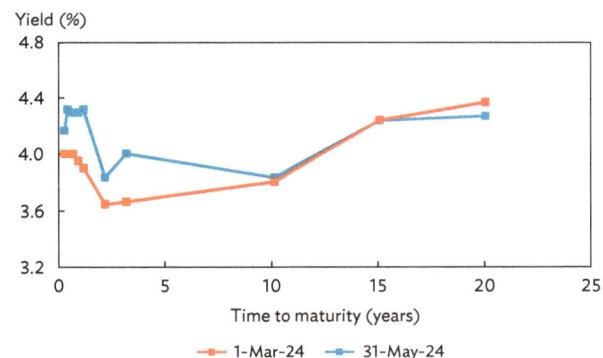

Source: Based on data from Bloomberg LP.

Figure 2: Composition of Local Currency Bonds Outstanding in Hong Kong, China

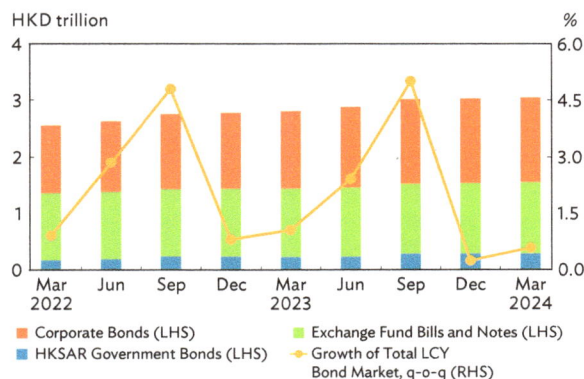

HKD = Hong Kong dollar, HKSAR = Hong Kong Special Administrative Region, LCY = local currency, LHS = left-hand side, q-o-q = quarter-on-quarter, RHS = right-hand side.
Source: Hong Kong Monetary Authority.

This market summary was written by Debbie Gundaya, consultant, Economic Research and Development Impact Department, ADB, Manila.

LCY bond issuance in Hong Kong, China rebounded in Q1 2024 from a contraction in the preceding quarter due to a recovery in corporate bond sales. Total LCY bond issuance tallied HKD1.3 trillion in Q1 2024, posting 2.9% q-o-q growth, a reversal from the decline in the fourth quarter of 2023 (**Figure 3**). Growth was driven solely by the robust issuance of corporate bonds, which expanded 34.8% q-o-q, on increased debt issuance by several state-owned entities. These issuances included the Airport Authority Hong Kong's inaugural retail bonds worth HKD5.0 billion and Hong Kong Mortgage Corporation's benchmark bonds totaling HKD12.0 billion. Meanwhile, issuance of HKSAR government bonds and Exchange Fund Bills and Notes contracted in Q1 2024. HKSAR government bond sales included HKD2.0 billion of 2-year digital green bonds issued to global institutional investors in February.[14]

Sustainable Bond Market

Outstanding sustainable bonds in Hong Kong, China are dominated by green bonds and public sector issuances. These bonds typically have short-term maturities and are denominated in foreign currency. Hong Kong, China's sustainable bonds outstanding reached a size of USD43.4 billion at the end of March, of which about 80% were green bonds and about 10% were social bonds (**Figure 4**). Outstanding sustainable bonds posted a nominal 0.3% q-o-q contraction in Q1 2024 as issuance declined 62.2% q-o-q to USD1.1 billion. Only green bond instruments were issued in Q1 2024. Most sustainable bonds are primarily issued by the government (61.4%) and have maturities of up to 5 years (71.7%). A large share of both government (42.8%) and private (37.2%) sustainable bonds are concentrated in tenors of 1–3 years. As a result, the size-weighted average tenor of Hong Kong, China's sustainable bonds at the end of Q1 2024 was 4.4 years, one of the lowest averages among all ASEAN+3 economies.[15] Foreign-currency-denominated instruments comprised over three-quarters of Hong Kong, China's sustainable bonds at the end of March.

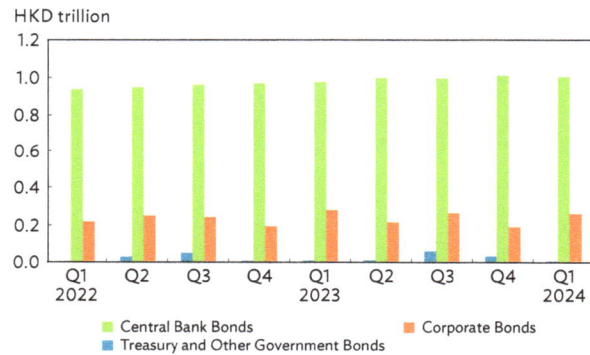

Figure 3: Composition of Local Currency Bond Issuance in Hong Kong, China

HKD trillion

Legend:
- Central Bank Bonds
- Corporate Bonds
- Treasury and Other Government Bonds

HKD = Hong Kong dollar, Q1 = first quarter, Q2 = second quarter, Q3 = third quarter, Q4 = fourth quarter.

Source: Hong Kong Monetary Authority.

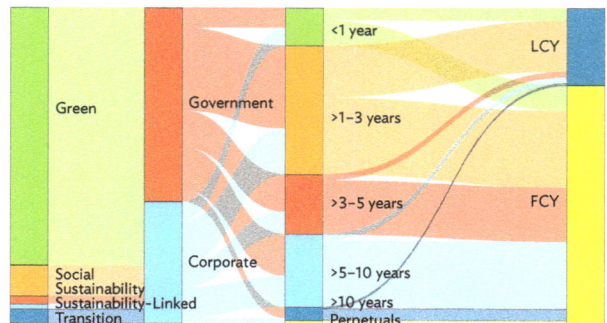

Figure 4: Market Profile of Outstanding Sustainable Bonds in Hong Kong, China at the End of March 2024

FCY = foreign currency, LCY = local currency.

Source: *AsianBondsOnline* calculations based on Bloomberg LP data.

---

[14] The HKD2.0 billion tranche of HKD-denominated bonds was part of a multicurrency digital green bond issuance, which also included CNY1.5 billion, USD200.0 million, and EUR80.0 million tranches.

[15] ASEAN+3 is defined to include member states of the Association of Southeast Asian Nations (ASEAN) plus the People's Republic of China; Hong Kong, China; Japan; and the Republic of Korea.

Indonesia

Yield Movements

Local currency (LCY) sovereign bond yields in Indonesia climbed an average of 31 basis points from 1 March to 31 May (Figure 1). The uptick in yields was largely driven by Bank Indonesia's 25 basis points policy rate hike to 6.25% on 24 April to safeguard the currency and ensure inflation remained within the target range of 1.5%–3.5% in 2024. Foreign bond outflows from Indonesia's bond market also pushed up yields amid a delay in the United States Federal Reserve's expected policy rate cut. In the first 4 months of the year, bond outflows reached USD3.2 billion, with March (USD1.6 billion) and April (USD1.3 billion) recording the largest outflows so far this year.

Figure 1: Indonesia's Benchmark Yield Curve—Local Currency Government Bonds

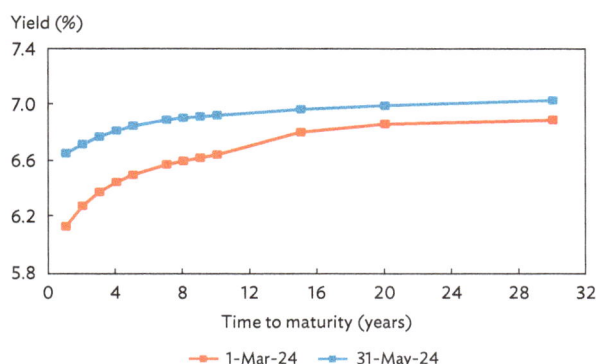

Source: Based on data from Bloomberg LP.

Local Currency Bond Market Size and Issuance

Growth in Indonesia's LCY bond market was capped by a high volume of maturities in the first quarter (Q1) of 2024. The LCY bond market in Indonesia reached a size of IDR6,786.5 trillion at the end of March, representing 19.4% of ASEAN's LCY bond market (**Figure 2**). Overall growth moderated to 3.1% quarter-on-quarter (q-o-q) in

Figure 2: Composition of Local Currency Bonds Outstanding in Indonesia

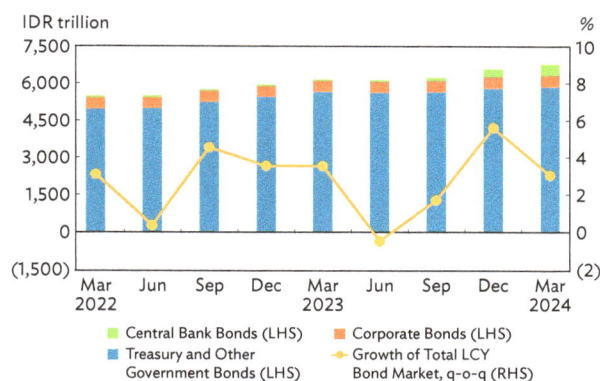

( ) = negative, IDR = Indonesian rupiah, LCY = local currency, LHS = left-hand side, q-o-q = quarter-on-quarter, RHS = right-hand side.
Notes: Data include *sukuk* (Islamic bonds). Data for Treasury and other government bonds comprise tradable and nontradable central government bonds.
Sources: Bank Indonesia; Directorate General of Budget Financing and Risk Management, Ministry of Finance; and Indonesia Stock Exchange.

Q1 2024 from 5.6% q-o-q in the previous quarter due to a high volume of maturities. Government bonds, which comprised 86.5% of Indonesia's LCY bond market, grew by only 1.1% q-o-q in Q1 2024 despite robust issuance during the quarter. On the other hand, corporate bonds, which accounted for 6.8% of total bonds at the end of March, posted a marginal contraction of 0.2% q-o-q due to a slowdown in issuance.

LCY bond issuance in Indonesia marginally contracted in Q1 2024 due to slower issuance by the central bank and corporates. Total issuance tallied IDR677.4 trillion in Q1 2024 for a 0.6% q-o-q contraction, reversing the 42.7% q-o-q hike in the preceding quarter (**Figure 3**). Government bond issuance surged 46.8% q-o-q as the government normally frontloads issuance in the first half of the year. In contrast, corporate bond issuance contracted amid still elevated interest rates. The three largest corporate bond issuers during the quarter were Tower Bersama Infrastructure, Sarana Multigriya Finansial, and Bank Rakyat Indonesia, which accounted for 10.6%, 10.4%, and 9.8%, respectively, of corporate bond issuance in Q1 2024.

This market summary was written by Roselyn Regalado, consultant, Economic Research and Development Impact Department, ADB, Manila.

Figure 3: Composition of Local Currency Bond Issuance in Indonesia

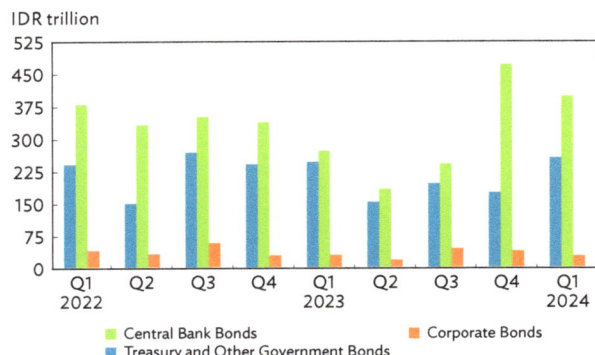

IDR = Indonesian rupiah, Q1 = first quarter, Q2 = second quarter, Q3 = third quarter, Q4 = fourth quarter.

Notes: Data include *sukuk* (Islamic bonds). Data for Treasury and other government bonds comprise tradable and nontradable central government bonds.

Sources: Bank Indonesia; Directorate General of Budget Financing and Risk Management, Ministry of Finance; and Indonesia Stock Exchange.

Investor Profile

The majority of LCY tradable government bonds in Indonesia were held by domestic investors, who accounted for a collective share of 85.8% at the end of March 2024. Domestic investors held 82.7% of conventional bonds outstanding, while their holdings share was much higher for Islamic bonds at 98.7% (**Figure 4**). Banking institutions remained the largest domestic investor group in both conventional and Islamic bonds, holding an overall share of 24.8%, albeit

down from 31.9% a year earlier. The decline was partly driven by the expansion in the central bank's holdings share from 18.3% to 21.3% during the same period, reflecting Bank Indonesia's ongoing support for the LCY bond market amid market volatility and portfolio outflows. Foreign investors exited Indonesia's bond market over a strengthening United States dollar, leading to a decline in their shareholdings from 14.9% at the end of March 2023 to 14.2% at the end of March 2024.

Sustainable Bond Market

A majority of sustainable bonds in Indonesia were green bond instruments, issued by the public sector, and carried long-term tenors. Green bonds comprised 81.7% of Indonesia's USD11.8 billion sustainable bonds outstanding at the end of March (**Figure 5**). The size of sustainable bond market, however, contracted a marginal 1.3% q-o-q as issuance declined by three-fold to USD0.4 billion in Q1 2024. The public sector played a significant role in Indonesia's sustainable bond market, representing 66.0% of its total sustainable bonds outstanding, and its active participation has contributed toward a longer maturity structure for sustainable bonds in the market. About 80.7% of the public sector's sustainable bonds carried maturities of over 5 years, while the corresponding share was only 34.7% for the private sector. As a result, the size-weighted average tenor of Indonesia's outstanding sustainable bonds stood at 7.5 years versus a size-weighted average of 4.2 years for ASEAN+3 economies.[16]

Figure 4: Investor Profile of Tradable Central Government Bonds

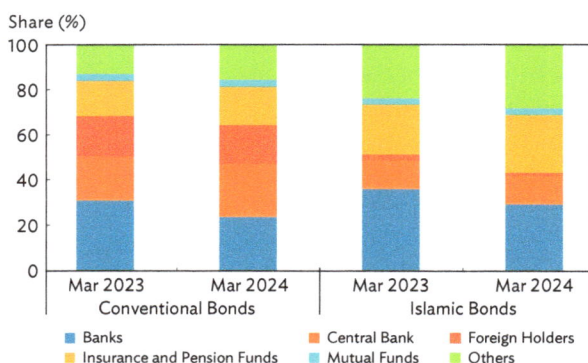

Source: Directorate General of Budget Financing and Risk Management, Ministry of Finance.

Figure 5: Market Profile of Outstanding Sustainable Bonds in Indonesia at the End of March 2024

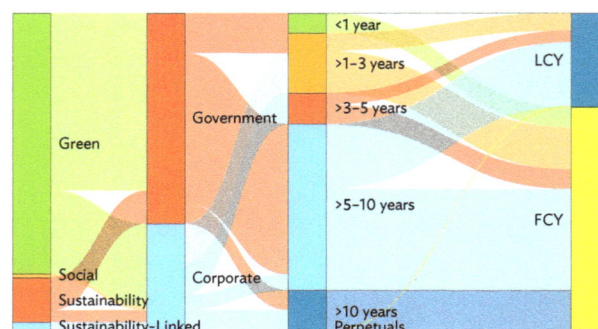

FCY = foreign currency, LCY = local currency.
Source: *AsianBondsOnline* calculations based on Bloomberg LP data.

---

[16] ASEAN+3 is defined to include member states of the Association of Southeast Asian Nations (ASEAN) plus the People's Republic of China; Hong Kong, China; Japan; and the Republic of Korea.

Republic of Korea

Yield Movements

Local currency (LCY) government bond yields in the Republic of Korea rose for most tenors between 1 March and 31 May due to a delay in the expected rate cut by the Bank of Korea (BOK) and the United States Federal Reserve. Yields rose a marginal 6 basis points on average for maturities of 3 years and longer, but fell at the short-end of the curve (with the exception of the 6-month tenor), during the review period (**Figure 1**). Market expectations of a rate cut this year were tempered following the BOK's 24 May monetary policy meeting when it left the base rate unchanged at 3.50% for an 11th straight meeting, stating that the increased upside risks to inflation still do not justify a rate cut. While inflation has slowed, upside risks have increased due to an improvement in economic growth and heightened foreign exchange volatility. Consequently, the BOK, in its 24 May meeting, raised the 2024 annual growth forecast to 2.5% from the February forecast of 2.1%, but maintained its inflation forecast at 2.6%. The delay in the United States Federal Reserve's rate cut also contributed to the rise in yields in the Republic of Korea's government bond market during the review period.

Figure 1: The Republic of Korea's Benchmark Yield Curve—Local Currency Government Bonds

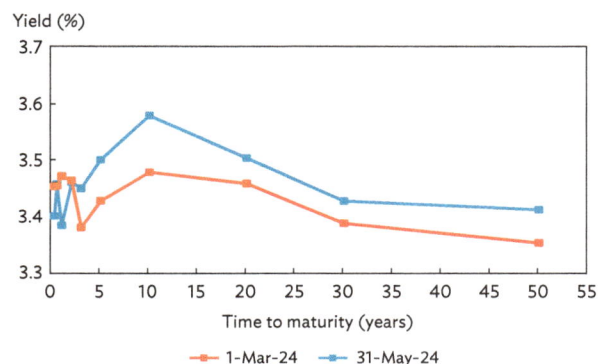

Source: Based on data from Bloomberg LP.

Local Currency Bond Market Size and Issuance

LCY bonds outstanding in the Republic of Korea rose 1.6% quarter-on-quarter (q-o-q) to reach KRW3,269.3 trillion at the end of March, driven by growth in both the government and corporate bond segments. The Republic of Korea's government bond market rose 1.6% q-o-q in the first quarter (Q1) of 2024, a rebound from the 0.3% q-o-q decline in the previous quarter, driven by increased issuance of Treasury bonds (**Figure 2**). Meanwhile, corporate bonds outstanding grew 1.8% q-o-q, despite the decline in issuance, due to a small volume of maturities.

Figure 2: Composition of Local Currency Bonds Outstanding in the Republic of Korea

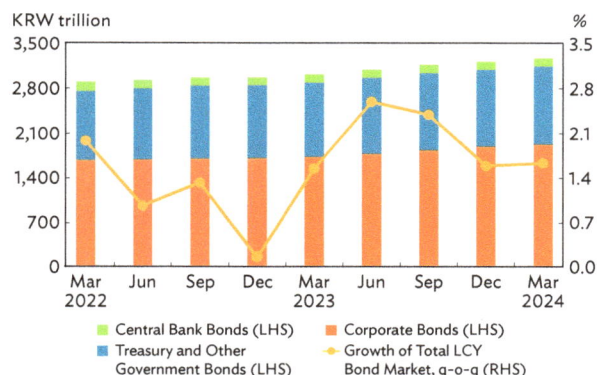

KRW = Korean won, LCY = local currency, LHS = left-hand side, q-o-q = quarter-on-quarter, RHS = right-hand side.
Sources: Bank of Korea and KG Zeroin Corp.

Total LCY bond issuance fell 13.0% q-o-q to KRW259.8 trillion in Q1 2024, dragged down by a contraction in the corporate bond segment. Issuance of corporate bonds dropped 24.4% q-o-q in Q1 2024 due to the rise in domestic yields being driven by the delay in the Federal Reserve's expected rate cut (**Figure 3**). Meanwhile, issuance of government bonds jumped 39.6% q-o-q due to the government's plan to finance the spending of more than 65% of the 2024 budget during the first half of the year.

This market summary was written by Angelica Andrea Cruz, consultant, Economic Research and Development Impact Department, ADB, Manila.

Figure 3: Composition of Local Currency Bond Issuance in the Republic of Korea

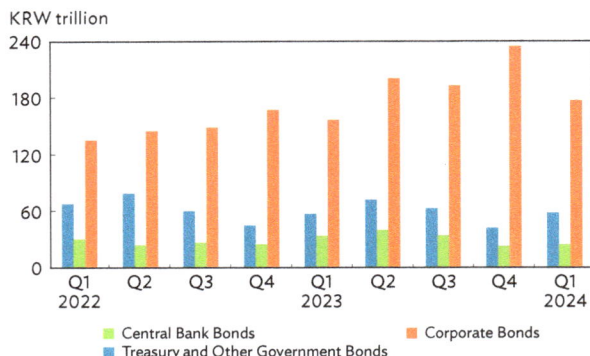

KRW = Korean won, Q1 = first quarter, Q2 = second quarter, Q3 = third quarter, Q4 = fourth quarter.
Sources: Bank of Korea and KG Zeroin Corp.

Investor Profile

Insurance companies and pension funds remained the largest investor group in the Republic of Korea's LCY bond market in 2023. The group held a collective share of 29.8% of total LCY bonds outstanding at the end of December, slightly lower than the 30.8% share in December 2022. In the government bond market, insurance companies and pension funds held a share of 29.8%, while banks and foreign investors were the next two largest investor groups with shares of 20.5% and 19.7%, respectively (**Figure 4**). The corporate bond

Figure 4: Local Currency Bonds Outstanding Investor Profile

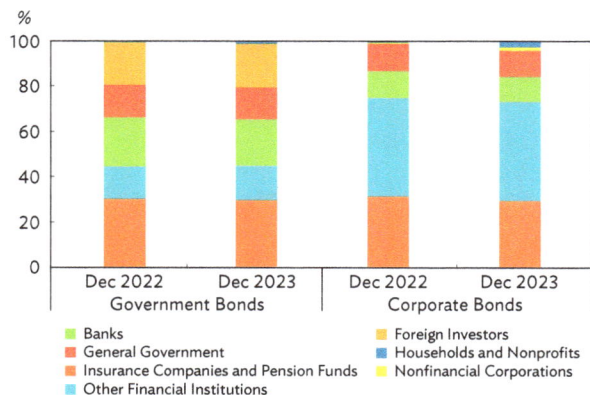

Sources: *AsianBondsOnline* and Bank of Korea.

market has a less diverse investor profile, with two major investor groups—other financial institutions (43.5%) and insurance companies and pension funds (29.6%)—continuing to hold almost three-quarters of total LCY corporate bonds outstanding. Foreign holdings in the LCY corporate bond market remained negligible at the end of December 2023.

Sustainable Bond Market

Nearly half of sustainable bonds outstanding in the Republic of Korea were social bonds, while bonds issued by the corporate sector and those carrying tenors of over 1 year to 3 years comprised a majority of total sustainable bonds outstanding at the end of March (Figure 5). The Republic of Korea's sustainable bond market reached a size of USD172.8 billion at the end of March, making it the second-largest sustainable bond market in emerging East Asia.[17] Social bonds comprised 48.9% of the sustainable bond market, followed by green bonds with a 31.8% share. Over half (56.3%) of the overall sustainable bond market comprised issuances by the corporate sector, while the government was the primary issuer of social bonds. About two-thirds of the sustainable bond stock had maturities of 3 years or less, resulting in a weighted average tenor of 3.0 years.

Figure 5: Market Profile of Outstanding Sustainable Bonds in the Republic of Korea at the End of March 2024

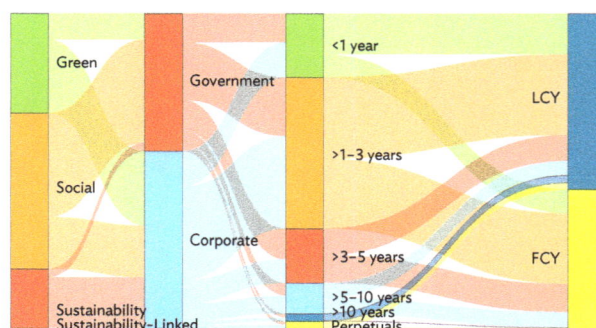

FCY = foreign currency, LCY = local currency.
Source: *AsianBondsOnline* calculations based on Bloomberg LP data.

[17] Emerging East Asia is defined to include member states of the Association of Southeast Asian Nations (ASEAN) plus the People's Republic of China; Hong Kong, China; and the Republic of Korea.

Malaysia

Yield Movements

Between 1 March and 31 May, the local currency (LCY) government bond yield curve of Malaysia shifted upward largely due to a delay in the expected rate cut by the United States Federal Reserve this year (Figure 1). In addition, Bank Negara Malaysia left its overnight policy rate unchanged at 3.00% on 9 May amid expectations of strong economic growth and moderate inflationary pressures. Malaysia's economy recorded 4.2% year-on-year (y-o-y) growth in the first quarter (Q1) of 2024, accelerating from 3.0% y-o-y in the previous quarter. Consumer price inflation in April remained stable at 1.8% y-o-y, the same rate as in February and March.

Local Currency Bond Market Size and Issuance

At the end of March, Malaysia's LCY bond market was valued at MYR2.0 trillion, an expansion of 1.7% quarter-on-quarter (q-o-q), supported by growth in Treasury and other government bonds, and corporate bonds (Figure 2). Malaysia saw a 3.2% q-o-q increase in outstanding Treasury and other government bonds in Q1 2024, led mainly by an expansion in the stock of government bonds. Meanwhile, outstanding corporate bonds increased slightly by 0.2% q-o-q due to less maturities during the quarter. By the end of March, DanaInfra Nasional remained the leading issuer of corporate securities with outstanding bonds amounting to MYR83.0 billion. *Sukuk* (Islamic bonds) increased 1.6% q-o-q and continued to comprise a majority of Malaysia's LCY bond market.

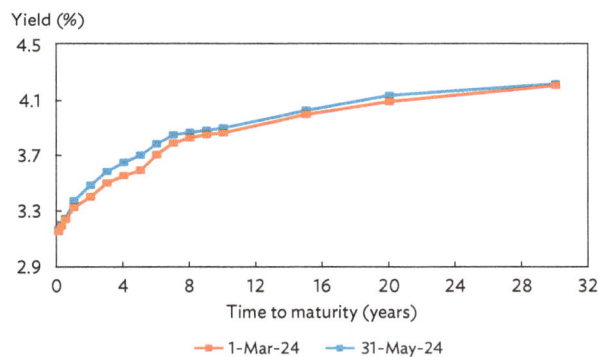

Figure 1: Malaysia's Benchmark Yield Curve—Local Currency Government Bonds

Source: Based on data from Bloomberg LP.

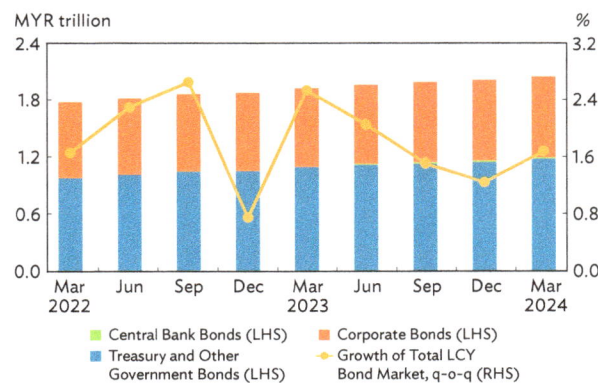

Figure 2: Composition of Local Currency Bonds Outstanding in Malaysia

LCY = local currency, LHS = left-hand side, MYR = Malaysian ringgit, q-o-q = quarter-on-quarter, RHS = right-hand side.
Source: Bank Negara Malaysia Fully Automated System for Issuing/Tendering.

This market summary was written by Patrick Vincent Lubenia, consultant, Economic Research and Development Impact Department, ADB, Manila.

Issuance of LCY bonds in Malaysia contracted 12.8% q-o-q in Q1 2024 on less issuance by corporates and the central bank (Figure 3). This marked the second consecutive quarterly contraction in issuance of Malaysian LCY bonds after recording a 12.2% q-o-q decline in the previous quarter. Issuance of corporate bonds fell 21.5% q-o-q, while Government Investment Issues (Islamic bonds) fell 2.4% q-o-q. On the other hand, Malaysian Government Securities (conventional bonds) increased 22.0% q-o-q, a rebound from the contraction of 24.0% q-o-q in the fourth quarter of 2023. During the review period, Maybank Islamic issued the largest amount of LCY bonds with eight Islamic commercial paper issuances totaling MYR4.0 billion.

Investor Profile

Malaysia's LCY government bonds' investor profile remained stable in 2023. Financial institutions, social security institutions, insurance companies, and foreign holders continued to dominate the LCY government bond market in 2023, collectively accounting for 90.2% of the total holdings at the end of December (**Figure 4**).

Sustainable Bond Market

At the end of March, corporate bonds dominated Malaysia's sustainable bond market, which mainly comprises sustainability bonds and long-term securities. Outstanding sustainable bonds in Malaysia totaled USD13.1 billion at the end of March, 75.9% of which were sustainability bonds amounting to USD9.9 billion, followed by green bonds at 18.8% and worth USD2.5 billion (**Figure 5**). However, this was lower compared with the sustainable bond stock at the end of December due to a contraction in issuance in Q1 2024. At the end of March, 73.9% of sustainable bonds were issued by private corporations, a majority of which carried tenors greater than 5 years. Meanwhile, all sustainable bonds from the public sector were in maturities longer than 5 years at the end of March. This led to a size-weighted average tenor of 8.8 years for all outstanding sustainable bonds in the Malaysian market. About four-fifths of the sustainable bonds outstanding in Malaysia were denominated in ringgit.

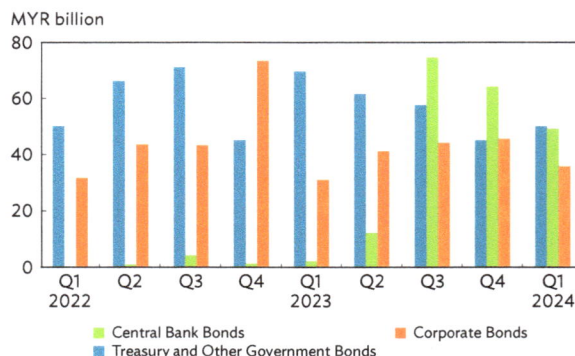

Figure 3: Composition of Local Currency Bond Issuance in Malaysia

MYR = Malaysian ringgit, Q1 = first quarter, Q2 = second quarter, Q3 = third quarter, Q4 = fourth quarter.
Source: Bank Negara Malaysia Fully Automated System for Issuing/Tendering.

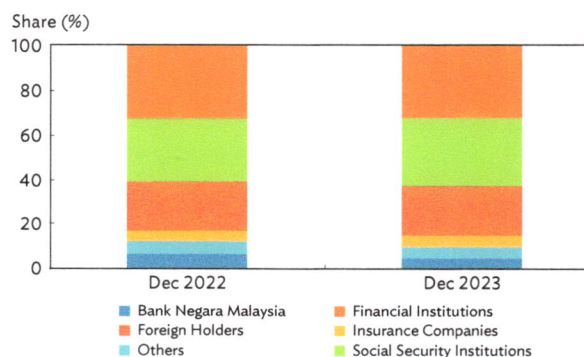

Figure 4: Local Currency Government Bonds Investor Profile

MYR = Malaysian ringgit.
Note: "Others" include statutory bodies, nominees and trustee companies, and cooperatives and unclassified items.
Source: Bank Negara Malaysia.

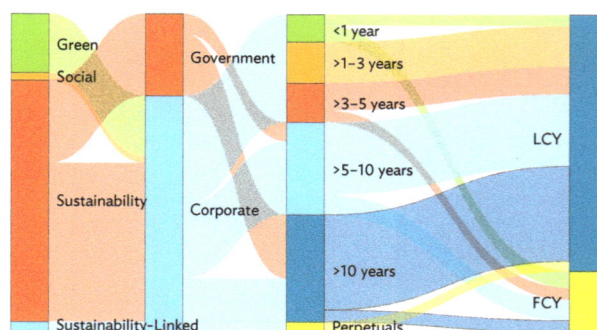

Figure 5: Market Profile of Outstanding Sustainable Bonds in Malaysia at the End of March 2024

FCY = foreign currency, LCY = local currency.
Source: *AsianBondsOnline* calculations based on Bloomberg LP data.

Philippines

Yield Movements

Local currency (LCY) government bond yields in the Philippines rose for most tenors between 1 March and 31 May, influenced by higher-for-longer interest rates—due to the United States Federal Reserve delaying its rate cut—and an uptick in domestic inflation (Figure 1). Year-on-year inflation continued to rise from 3.7% in March to 3.8% in April and 3.9% in May. While inflation had settled within the government's target range of 2%–4% for 6 consecutive months, the Bangko Sentral ng Pilipinas (BSP), in its 16 May policy meeting, opted to keep its overnight reverse repurchase rate steady at a 17-year high of 6.50%. The central bank's decision aims to firmly anchor inflation expectations within the target range amid persistent potential price pressures linked to higher costs of transportation, food, and energy, as well as rising global oil prices. In a press event on 16 May, BSP Governor Eli M. Remolona Jr. hinted at a possible rate cut in August.

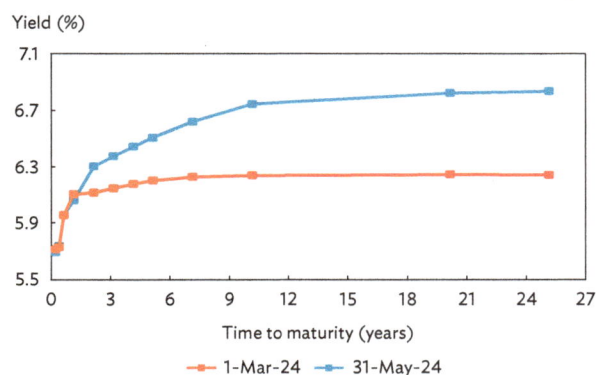

Figure 1: The Philippines' Benchmark Yield Curve— Local Currency Government Bonds

Source: Based on data from Bloomberg LP.

Local Currency Bond Market Size and Issuance

Growth in the Philippines' LCY bond market picked up in the first quarter (Q1) of 2024, with bonds outstanding reaching a size of PHP12.3 trillion at the end of March. Overall growth climbed 2.2% quarter-on-quarter (q-o-q) in Q1 2024 from 1.0% q-o-q in the fourth quarter of 2023 due to increased issuance from

the government and the BSP (**Figure 2**). Treasury and other government bonds outstanding posted growth of 2.7% q-o-q and the stock of central bank securities rose 20.2% q-o-q in Q1 2024. However, corporate bonds outstanding continued to decline in Q1 2024 at a pace of 8.2% q-o-q due to a large number of maturities and a low volume of issuance during the quarter.

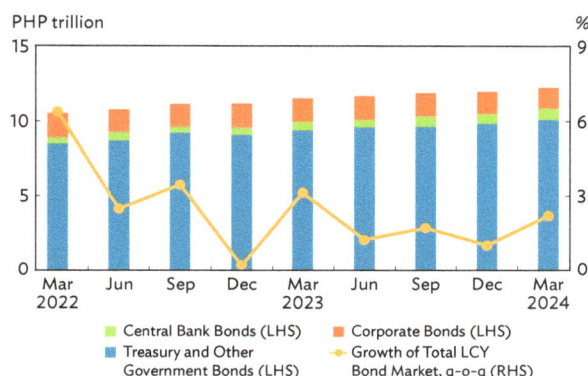

Figure 2: Composition of Local Currency Bonds Outstanding in the Philippines

LCY = local currency, LHS = left-hand side, PHP = Philippine peso, q-o-q = quarter-on-quarter, RHS = right-hand side.
Note: Treasury and other government bonds comprise Treasury bonds, Treasury bills, and bonds issued by government agencies, entities, and corporations for which repayment is guaranteed by the Government of the Philippines. This includes bonds issued by Power Sector Assets and Liabilities Management and the National Food Authority, among others.
Sources: Bureau of the Treasury and Bloomberg LP.

LCY bond issuance rebounded with growth of 37.3% q-o-q in Q1 2024 for a total of PHP3.1 trillion, reversing a contraction of 4.4% q-o-q in the fourth quarter of 2023. The increase in overall issuance was largely driven by Treasury and other government bonds, whose issuance expanded almost threefold to PHP1.2 trillion from the previous quarter's PHP0.4 trillion, as the government frontloaded its issuance for the year (**Figure 3**). Issuance of government bonds in Q1 2024 was further buoyed by the sale of Retail Treasury Bonds in February amounting to PHP584.9 billion. On the other hand, due to the elevated interest rate environment, corporate bond issuance dipped 0.1% q-o-q during the quarter, with only two firms tapping the bond market: BDO Unibank (PHP63.3 billion) and Filinvest Development Corporation (PHP10.0 billion).

Figure 3: Composition of Local Currency Bond Issuance in the Philippines

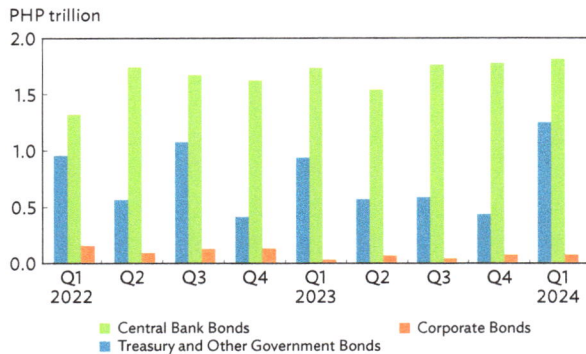

PHP trillion

PHP = Philippine peso, Q1 = first quarter, Q2 = second quarter, Q3 = third quarter, Q4 = fourth quarter.

Note: Treasury and other government bonds comprise Treasury bonds, Treasury bills, and bonds issued by government agencies, entities, and corporations for which repayment is guaranteed by the Government of the Philippines. This includes bonds issued by Power Sector Assets and Liabilities Management and the National Food Authority, among others.

Sources: Bureau of the Treasury and Bloomberg LP.

Investor Profile

Banks and investment houses, as well as contractual savings institutions and tax-exempt institutions, remained the primary holders of LCY government bonds at the end of March 2024. Their combined bond holdings comprised about 80% of the market's total LCY government debt stock (**Figure 4**). Banks and investment

Figure 4: Investor Profile of Local Currency Government Bonds

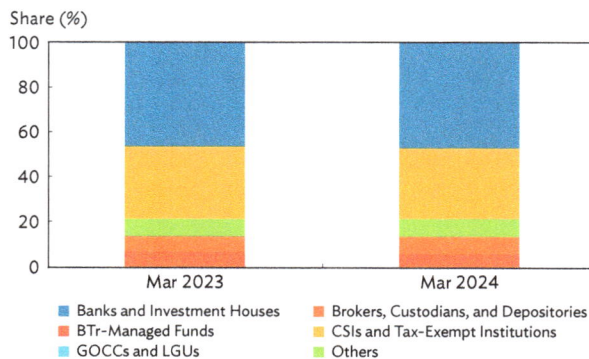

Share (%)

BTr = Bureau of the Treasury, CSI = contractual savings institution, GOCC = government-owned or -controlled corporation, LGU = local government unit.

Note: At the end of March 2024, government-owned or -controlled corporations and local government units' holdings share was 0.02%, amounting to PHP2.2 billion.

Source: Bureau of the Treasury.

houses remained the single-largest investor group, with investment holdings inching up to a share of 47.0% from 46.4% in March 2023, followed by contractual savings institutions (31.4%). Overall, the investor landscape in the Philippines' LCY government bond market at the end of March 2024 was largely unchanged from a year earlier.

Sustainable Bond Market

Sustainable bonds in the Philippines are mainly sustainability bond instruments issued by the government and corporates (**Figure 5**). Sustainability bonds accounted for 72.5% of the economy's total sustainable bonds at the end of March, with most denominated in foreign currency and carrying a tenor of over 5 years. Due to the resumption of issuance by corporates, the amount of sustainable bonds outstanding grew 2.0% q-o-q in Q1 2024 to USD8.5 billion, more than half of which came from the corporate sector. About 89.1% of sustainable bonds from the government carried maturities of over 5 years, while the corporate sector's corresponding share was only 32.6%, resulting in a size-weighted average tenor of 11.1 years.

Figure 5: Market Profile of Outstanding Sustainable Bonds in the Philippines at the End of March 2024

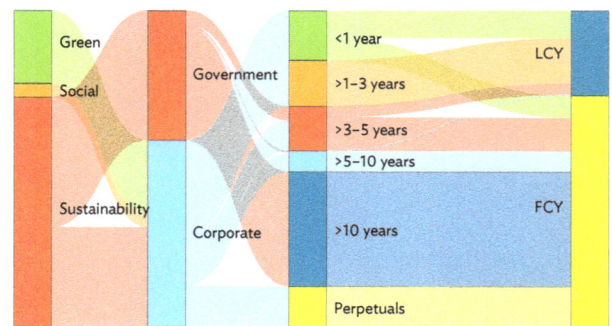

FCY = foreign currency, LCY = local currency.

Source: *AsianBondsOnline* calculations based on Bloomberg LP data.

Singapore

Yield Movements

Between 1 March and 31 May, government bond yields in Singapore increased by 21 basis points on average, except for short-end tenors, due to delays in the expected rate cuts by the United States Federal Reserve (**Figure 1**). Yields with tenors 1 year and above rose, tracking the yield curve movement of United States Treasuries, while yields on short-term tenors were slightly down. In April, the Monetary Authority of Singapore kept its monetary policy stance unchanged by maintaining the rate of appreciation of the Singapore dollar's nominal effective exchange rate amid a positive economic growth outlook and easing inflationary pressure. Singapore's economy grew 2.7% year-on-year (y-o-y) in the first quarter (Q1) of 2024, accelerating from 2.2% y-o-y in the prior quarter, and consumer price inflation remained at 2.7% y-o-y in March and April, down from 3.4% y-o-y in February.

Local Currency Bond Market Size and Issuance

The local currency (LCY) bond market of Singapore expanded 2.7% quarter-on-quarter (q-o-q), reaching SGD734.8 billion at the end of March (**Figure 2**). Central bank bills, which continued to dominate the LCY bond market in Singapore, grew 4.7% q-o-q due to fewer securities maturing during the quarter. Corporations also contributed to the quarterly growth of Singapore's LCY bond market as the stock of outstanding LCY corporate bonds increased 1.6% q-o-q. Government-owned Housing & Development Board had the most outstanding LCY corporate bonds at the end of March, amounting to SGD28.6 billion.

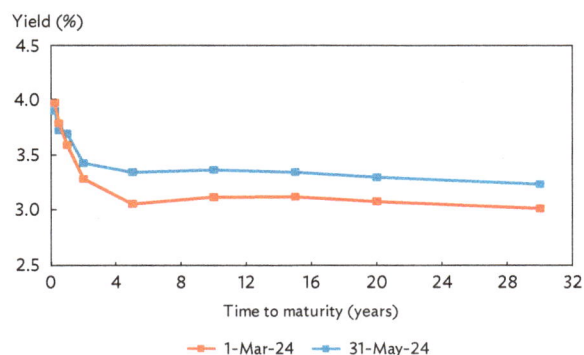

Figure 1: Singapore's Benchmark Yield Curve— Local Currency Government Bonds

Source: Based on data from Bloomberg LP.

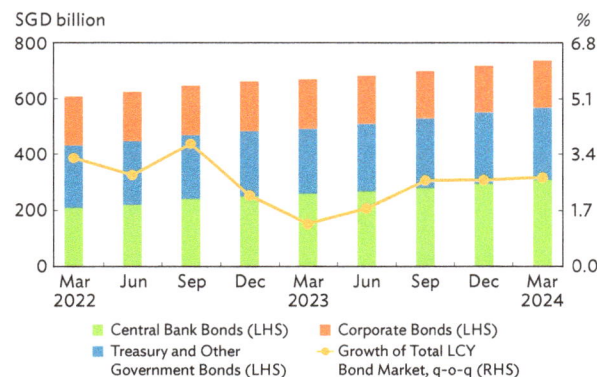

Figure 2: Composition of Local Currency Bonds Outstanding in Singapore

LCY = local currency, LHS = left-hand side, q-o-q = quarter-on-quarter, RHS = right-hand side, SGD = Singapore dollar.
Note: Corporate bonds are based on *AsianBondsOnline* estimates.
Sources: Monetary Authority of Singapore and Bloomberg LP.

LCY bond issuance contracted 1.1% q-o-q in Q1 2024 on declining issuance of central bank bills (Figure 3). The issuance of Monetary Authority of Singapore bills and notes declined 2.6% q-o-q in Q1 2024. However, this was slightly offset by a rebound in the issuance of Treasury and other government bonds, which jumped 8.0% q-o-q. Issuance of LCY corporate bonds in Q1 2024 doubled from the previous quarter, albeit from a low base. Government-owned Housing & Development Board was the largest issuer during Q1 2024 with two fixed-income securities totaling SGD1.5 billion.

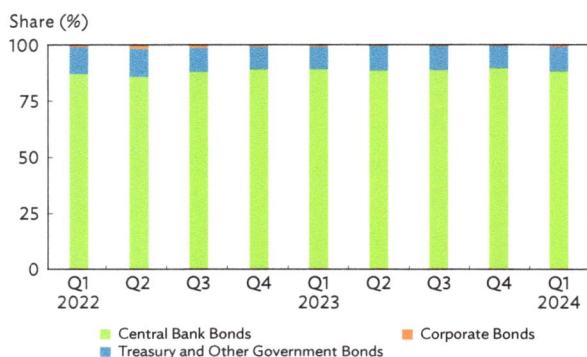

Figure 3: Composition of Local Currency Bond Issuance in Singapore

Q1 = first quarter, Q2 = second quarter, Q3 = third quarter, Q4 = fourth quarter, SGD = Singapore dollar.
Note: Corporate bonds are based on *AsianBondsOnline* estimates.
Sources: Monetary Authority of Singapore and Bloomberg LP.

Sustainable Bond Market

At the end of March, corporate issuances comprised most of Singapore's outstanding sustainable bonds, which were dominated by green bonds and longer-tenor securities. Of the total USD19.2 billion of sustainable bonds outstanding at the end of March, green bonds comprised the largest share by bond type at 79.0% (USD15.2 billion) (**Figure 4**). This was followed by sustainability-linked bonds at 11.4% (USD2.2 billion). Increased issuance of green and sustainability-linked bonds in Q1 2024 contributed to the 4.0% q-o-q expansion of Singapore's sustainable bond market by the end of March. Private sector bonds made up 58.3% of the outstanding sustainable bonds. The 41.7% share issued by public entities were purely green bonds. The Housing & Development Board issued the largest LCY corporate bond in Q1 2024 with an SGD800.0 million 5-year green bond that will be used to finance projects under the company's Green Finance Framework. About three-quarters of the outstanding sustainable bonds at the end of March were LCY-denominated. About 40% carried a tenor of more than 10 years, resulting in Singapore's outstanding sustainable bonds having a size-weighted average tenor of 16.6 years.

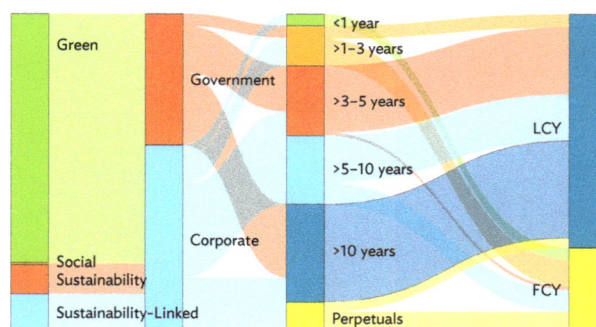

Figure 4: Market Profile of Outstanding Sustainable Bonds in Singapore at the End of March 2024

FCY = foreign currency, LCY = local currency.
Source: *AsianBondsOnline* calculations based on Bloomberg LP data.

Thailand

Yield Movements

Local currenty (LCY) government bond yields in Thailand rose for all maturities between 1 March and 31 May (Figure 1). Bond yields increased by an average of 22 basis points across all tenors as both the United States (US) Federal Reserve and the Bank of Thailand (BOT) maintained tight monetary policies during the review period. In its 30 April–1 May meeting, the Federal Reserve left its policy rate unchanged at 5.25%–5.50%, hinting that rates would remain elevated until inflation in the US sufficiently trended down toward its 2.0% target. Meanwhile, the BOT kept its policy rate at 2.50% at its 10 April meeting despite political pressure to lower rates, noting that monetary policy will have limited impact on structural issues affecting economic growth. Both central banks subsequently held their policy rates unchanged during their June monetary policy meetings.

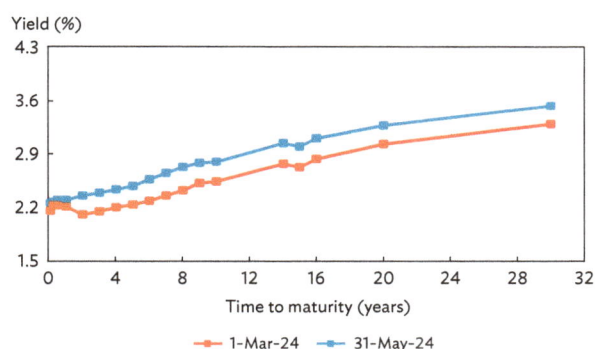

Figure 2: Composition of Local Currency Bonds Outstanding in Thailand

( ) = negative, LCY = local currency, LHS = left-hand side, q-o-q = quarter-on-quarter, RHS = right-hand side, THB = Thai baht.
Source: Bank of Thailand.

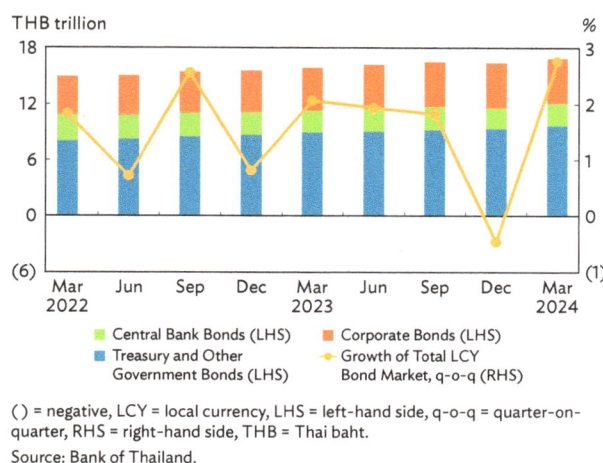

Figure 1: Thailand's Benchmark Yield Curve—Local Currency Government Bonds

Sources: Based on data from Bloomberg LP and Thai Bond Market Association.

Local Currency Bond Market Size and Issuance

Thailand's LCY bond market rebounded in the first quarter (Q1) of 2024, led by faster growth in government bonds. Outstanding LCY bonds totaled THB16.9 trillion at the end of March (**Figure 2**). This marked a 2.8% quarter-on-quarter (q-o-q) increase

in Q1 2024, following a 0.5% q-o-q contraction in the fourth quarter (Q4) of 2023. Growth in Treasury and other government bonds edged up to 3.9% q-o-q in Q1 2024 from 1.0% q-o-q in Q4 2023 due to a rebound in issuances. BOT bonds outstanding also recovered, growing 5.7% q-o-q in Q1 2024. In contrast, outstanding corporate bonds fell 0.9% q-o-q, as issuance continued to contract amid elevated interest rates. At the end of March, Treasury and other government bonds (57.7%) remained a majority of Thailand's LCY bond market, followed by corporate bonds (28.3%) and BOT bonds (13.9%).

LCY bond issuance in Thailand rebounded in Q1 2024, fueled by a recovery in government bond sales. LCY bond issuance (THB2.2 trillion) posted strong growth of 12.2% q-o-q in Q1 2024, recovering from an 11.3% q-o-q contraction in Q4 2023 (**Figure 3**). The growth was led by Treasury and other bond issuance, which expanded 33.9% q-o-q to THB654.0 billion in Q1 2024, as the government increased debt issuance to help finance the budget deficit for fiscal year 2024. BOT bond issuance also increased 11.9% q-o-q to THB1.2 trillion in Q1 2024. However, corporate bond sales contracted 10.3% q-o-q in Q1 2024 due to high borrowing rates and weak investor confidence amid the slow economic recovery.

This market summary was written by Debbie Gundaya, consultant, Economic Research and Development Impact Department, ADB, Manila.

Figure 3: Composition of Local Currency Bond Issuance in Thailand

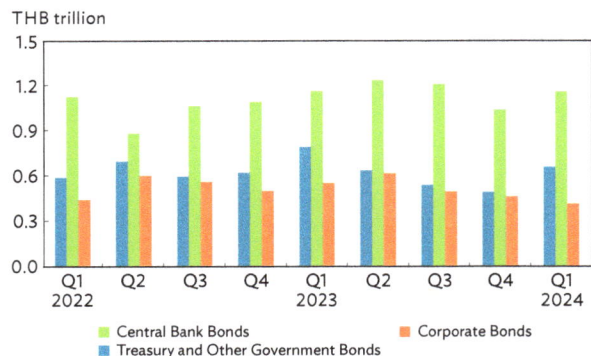

THB trillion

Q1 = first quarter, Q2 = second quarter, Q3 = third quarter, Q4 = fourth quarter, THB = Thai baht.
Source: Bank of Thailand.

Thai Beverage, Global Power Synergy, and CP ALL were the top three issuers of corporate debt in Q1 2024, with total issuances of THB22.0 billion, THB15.0 billion, and THB15.0 billion, respectively.

Investor Profile

Domestic investors held a majority of Thai LCY government bonds, with foreign holders' share falling below 10% at the end of March 2024. Domestic investors' share of LCY government bonds increased to 90.1% at the end of March, up from 87.7% a year earlier, driven by increased holdings among banks and mutual

funds. Meanwhile, foreign investors' holdings of Thai LCY government bonds declined to 9.9% from 12.3% during the same period, as interest rate differentials between US Treasury bonds and Thai bonds remained wide (**Figure 4**). The BOT's share of LCY government bond holdings was steady at 6.4% between March 2023 and March 2024.

Sustainable Bond Market

At the end of March, the sustainable bond market in Thailand primarily comprised sustainability bonds issued by the government. Government-issued sustainability bonds generally have long-term tenors and are denominated in Thai baht (**Figure 5**). The size of the sustainable bond market fell to USD19.4 billion at the end of March, contracting 1.9% q-o-q due to a slowdown in issuance during the quarter. Sustainability bonds comprised 67.0% of total sustainable bonds outstanding at the end of March, followed by green bonds (21.7%). Thailand's sustainable bond market is dominated by government bonds (68.9%), and over three-quarters (76.2%) carry maturities longer than 5 years. Over 90% of government sustainable bonds carry maturities longer than 10 years, while the largest share (32.3%) of corporate sustainable bonds have tenors of over 5 years to 10 years. As a result, the size-weighted average tenor of Thai sustainable bonds stood at 9.5 years at the end of March, the third-longest average among ASEAN+3 markets.[18] The majority of sustainable bonds are denominated in Thai baht, with only 0.4% denominated in a foreign currency.

Figure 4: Investor Profile of Government Bonds in Thailand

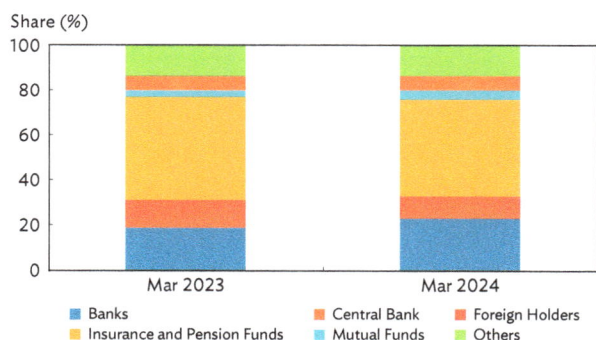

Share (%)

Source: Bank of Thailand.

Figure 5: Market Profile of Outstanding Sustainable Bonds in Thailand at the End of March 2024

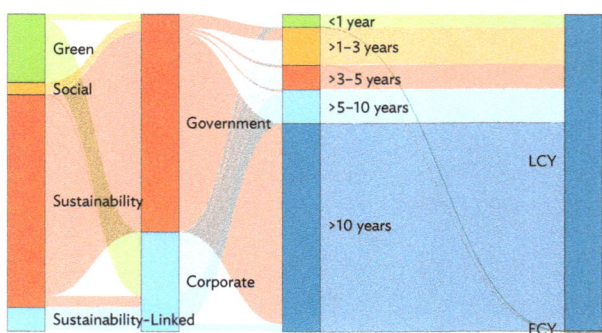

FCY = foreign currency, LCY = local currency.
Source: *AsianBondsOnline* calculations based on Bloomberg LP data.

---

[18] ASEAN+3 is defined to include member states of the Association of Southeast Asian Nations (ASEAN) plus the People's Republic of China; Hong Kong, China; Japan; and the Republic of Korea.

Viet Nam

Yield Movements

Local currency (LCY) government bond yields in Viet Nam rose for all tenors between 1 March and 31 May. Bond yields increased an average of 56 basis points due to the United States Federal Reserve's delay in cutting its policy rate and rising domestic inflation (**Figure 1**). Viet Nam's year-on-year (y-o-y) consumer price inflation inched up to 4.44% in May, driven by elevated energy and pork meat prices, edging closer to the government's 2024 ceiling of 4.50%. The May inflation reading was up from 4.40% y-o-y in April and 3.97% y-o-y in March, and was also the highest level since January 2023. While inflation remained within the government's target, mounting inflationary pressures loom due to wage hikes; soaring gold prices; the depreciation of the Vietnamese dong; and elevated costs in the healthcare, education, and electricity sectors.

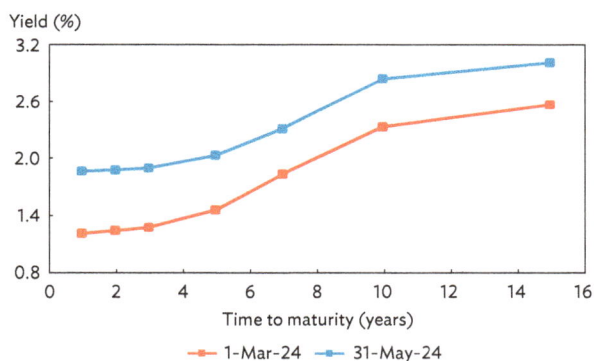

Figure 2: Composition of Local Currency Bonds Outstanding in Viet Nam

( ) = negative, LCY = local currency, LHS = left-hand side, q-o-q = quarter-on-quarter, RHS = right-hand side, VND = Vietnamese dong.
Note: Other government bonds comprise government-guaranteed and municipal bonds.
Sources: Vietnam Bond Market Association and Bloomberg LP.

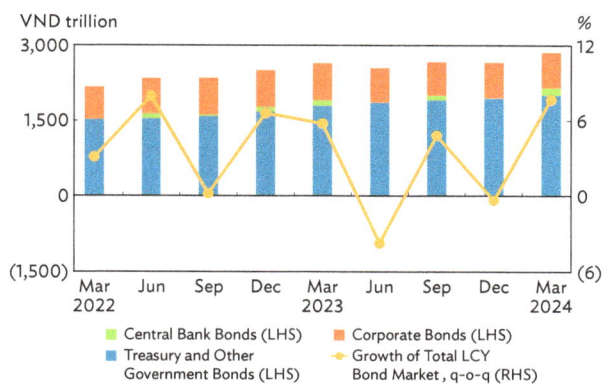

Figure 1: Viet Nam's Benchmark Yield Curve— Local Currency Government Bonds

Source: Based on data from Bloomberg LP.

Local Currency Bond Market Size and Issuance

Growth in Viet Nam's LCY bond market rebounded to 7.7% quarter-on-quarter (q-o-q) in the first quarter (Q1) of 2024. The LCY bond market's overall growth was driven by increased issuance from the

government and the State Bank of Vietnam's resumption of central bank bills issuance in March to support the Vietnamese dong. Treasury and other government bonds (VND2,004.2 trillion), which accounted for the majority of Viet Nam's total debt stock, grew 3.3% q-o-q in Q1 2024 on increased issuance to support the government's funding requirements (**Figure 2**). On the other hand, corporate bonds (VND709.7 trillion), which comprised 24.8% of the total LCY bond market at the end of March, contracted 0.9% q-o-q due to a large number of maturities and a low volume of issuance during the quarter.

LCY bond issuance fell 36.7% q-o-q in Q1 2024 on lower issuance from corporates and central bank (**Figure 3**). Corporate bond issuance contracted 81.3% q-o-q in Q1 2024, a reversal from the previous quarter's expansion of 74.5% q-o-q. This was due to the reinstitution of several provisions under Decree No. 65 at the beginning of 2024, following a period of suspension and postponement under Decree No. 8.[19] This change created challenges for corporate issuers due to difficulties in meeting the requirements of Decree No. 65. Meanwhile, central bank bill issuance contracted

---

This market summary was written by Jeremy Grace Ilustrisimo, consultant, Economic Research and Development Impact Department, ADB, Manila.

[19] Decree No. 8, which was issued by the Government of Viet Nam on 5 March 2023, suspended the following provisions under Decree No. 65 until 1 January 2024: (i) professional investor status requirement: an investor must hold a portfolio of securities valued at least VND2.0 billion for a minimum of 180 consecutive days; (ii) issuer credit ratings: an issuer's credit rating must be included in the bond issuance plan; and (iii) distribution of bonds must be completed within 30 days from the date of public disclosure of the issuance.

Figure 3: Composition of Local Currency Bond Issuance in Viet Nam

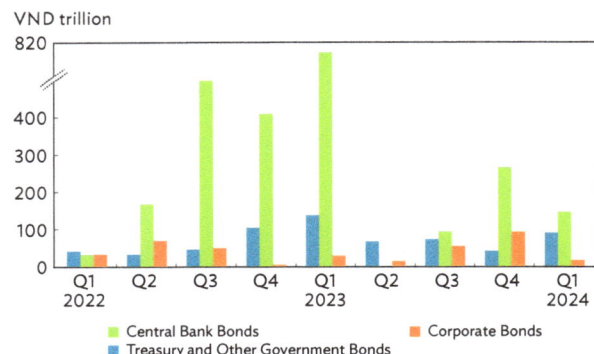

VND trillion

Q1 = first quarter, Q2 = second quarter, Q3 = third quarter, Q4 = fourth quarter, VND = Vietnamese dong.
Note: Other government bonds comprise government-guaranteed and municipal bonds.
Sources: Vietnam Bond Market Association and Bloomberg LP.

Figure 4: Profile of Two Dominant Investors for Local Currency Government Bonds

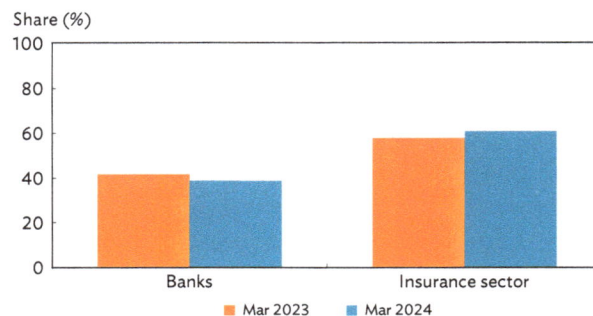

Share (%)

Source: Viet Nam Ministry of Finance.

45.2% q-o-q since the State Bank of Vietnam only resumed issuance during the last month of the quarter. At the same time, the issuance of Treasury and other government bonds increased more than twofold from the previous quarter to VND90.5 trillion.

Investor Profile

Nearly all government securities outstanding at the end of March 2024 were held by insurance firms and banks, accounting for a combined holdings share of 99.5%. Insurance companies remained the single-largest investor group, with their holdings share increasing to 60.8% in March 2024 from 57.8% a year earlier (**Figure 4**). Meanwhile, banks' holdings share decreased to 38.7% from 41.7% during the same period. The LCY government bond market in Viet Nam remained dominated by only two investor groups; as a result, Viet Nam continued to have the highest Herfindahl–Hirschman Index score among its regional peers.[20] Meanwhile, the cumulative holdings share of offshore investors, securities companies and investment funds, and other investors totaled 0.5%.

Sustainable Bond Market

The sustainable bond market in Viet Nam comprises green bonds and sustainable bond instruments issued solely by corporates and mostly carrying short-term tenors (Figure 5). Due to the absence of issuance during the quarter, the total stock of sustainable bonds contracted 0.5% q-o-q to a size of USD0.8 billion at the end of Q1 2024. More than half (53.4%) of the sustainable bond stock comprised sustainability bonds carrying maturities of 3 years or less, and the remaining 46.6% were green bonds, about 54.0% of which carried tenors of 3 years or less, resulting in a size-weighted average tenor of 3.2 years. Foreign-currency-denominated instruments comprised over 70.0% of the economy's total sustainable bonds at the end of March.

Figure 5: Market Profile of Outstanding Sustainable Bonds in Viet Nam at the End of March 2024

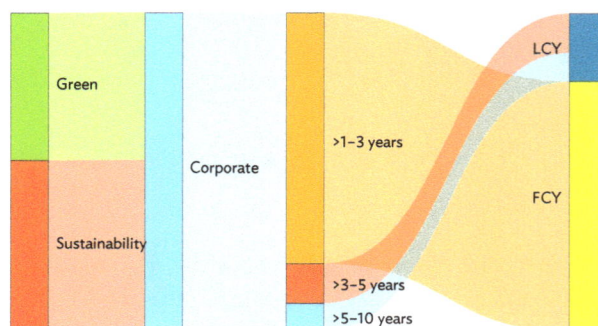

FCY = foreign currency, LCY = local currency.
Source: *AsianBondsOnline* calculations based on Bloomberg LP data.

[20] The Herfindahl–Hirschman Index is a commonly accepted measure of market concentration. In this case, the index is used to measure the investor profile diversification of the LCY bond market and is calculated by summing the squared share of each investor group in the bond market.

www.ingramcontent.com/pod-product-compliance
Lightning Source LLC
Chambersburg PA
CBHW042036220326
41599CB00045BA/7481